The
OLD HAND-KNITTERS
of the DALES

The OLD HAND-KNITTERS of the DALES

With an Introduction to the Early History of Knitting

Written and illustrated by
MARIE HARTLEY *and* JOAN INGILBY

*With a new foreword and patterns
by Penelope Lister Hemingway*

COOPERATIVE PRESS
Cleveland, Ohio

Library of Congress Control Number: 2013956115
ISBN 13 (print): 978-1-937513-26-9
ISBN 13 (e-book): 978-1-937513-51-1
First Cooperative Press Edition
Published by http://www.cooperativepress.com

Patterns, charts, photos, and new foreword ©2014 Penelope Lister Hemingway
Illustrations and original text ©1951 Marie Hartley and Joan Ingilby

Every effort has been made to ensure that all the information in this book is accurate at the time of publication; however, Cooperative Press neither endorses nor guarantees the content of external links referenced in this book.

If you have questions or comments about this book, or need information about licensing, custom editions, special sales, or academic/corporate purchases, please contact Cooperative Press: info@cooperativepress.com or 13000 Athens Ave C288, Lakewood, OH 44107 USA

No part of this book may be reproduced in any form, except brief excerpts for the purpose of review, without prior written permission of the publisher. Thank you for respecting our copyright.

For Cooperative Press

Senior Editor: Shannon Okey
Art Director / Assistant Editor: Elizabeth Green Musselman
Book Designer: Terri Hamilton
Technical Editor: Andi Smith

Publication History

The Old Hand-Knitters of the Dales was first published in 1951 by The Dalesman Publishing Company, Clapham, Yorkshire, 1951, by Harry J. Scott. The book was written in 1948/9, but remained unpublished for two years due to post-war paper shortages. The original illustrations are by Marie Hartley.

Many, many thanks are due to Thelma Bannister, Marie Hartley's niece, who gave permission to republish her aunt's work, and to Penelope Hemingway, whose Cooperative Press book *River Ganseys* set us on the path to republishing *The Old Hand-Knitters of the Dales*.

To Yorkshirefolk—and those who love knitting and history—everywhere.

TABLE OF CONTENTS

Illustrations ix

Foreword to the Revised Edition by Penelope Hemingway xi

The OLD HAND-KNITTERS *of the* DALES

Original Foreword 5

Chapter I—Knitting in Early Times..7

Chapter II—The Knitting Industry 13

Chapter III—The Old Hand-Knitters of the Dales 21

Chapter IV—Swaledale... 31
    1. The Yeoman Hosier 31
    2. The Last Phase 41

Chapter V—Wensleydale.. 45
    1. Askrigg 45
    2. Yore Mills, Aysgarth 55
    3. Gayle and Hawes 60

Chapter VI—Westmorland... 69
    1. Kendal 69
    2. Ravenstonedale and Orton.. 73
    3. Kirkby Stephen... 77

Chapter VII—The Terrible Knitters e' Dent 83

Chapter VIII—The Romance of Hebblethwaite Hall..................................... 95

APPENDICES

Appendix A—Knitting Sheaths 107
Appendix B—List of People Employed Latterly
   at Hebblethwaite Hall Mill 115
Appendix C—Cumberland Farmers from Whom J. Dover
   Bought Wool 116
Appendix D—List of Firms Mentioned in Hebblethwaite Hall Ledger....117
Appendix E—Joseph Dover's Letters 119
Appendix F (new to this edition)—The George Walton Gloves 141

Bibliography 183

ILLUSTRATIONS

PHOTOGRAPHS
Kilmarnock Cap and Coptic Objects
Knitters in Wensleydale (from Walker's *Costumes of Yorkshire*)
Betty and Kit Metcalfe
Dent child with cops
The Stocking Market, Kirkby Stephen, 1817
Dent Town, 1810
Martha Dinsdale
Dove Cottage gloves (first)
Dent gloves—tops, and palms
Dove Cottage gloves (second)—tops, and palms

LINE DRAWINGS
"The Terrible Knitters E' Dent"
Richmond
Patterned Gloves
Typical Dales Knitting Sheath
Sealhouses, Arkengarthdale
Hand cards from Arkengarthdale
Top Crook
Low Mill, Askrigg
Crane, Low Mill
Wool Comb
Yore Mills, Aysgarth
Spinning Wheel from Aysgarth
Hawes Mill
Gayle Mill
Spinning Gallery, Newbiggin-on-Lune
Spinning Gallery, Adamthwaite Farm
Kirkby Stephen Carrier
Gibbs Hall
Hebblethwaite Hall
17th and 18th Century Knitting Sheaths
A Collection of Local Knitting Sheaths
19th Century Knitting Sheaths
Knitting Sheaths of various materials
Highland Knitting Pad

FOREWORD TO THE REVISED EDITION
BY PENELOPE LISTER HEMINGWAY

> Writing this book in the late 1940s we glimpsed a way of life which in spite of the Industrial Revolution, had remained unchanged for centuries. Since then the picture has faded rapidly; and as the years pass, by the round of any oral tradition, becomes faint, soon perhaps to cease altogether.
> —*Fifty Years in the Yorkshire Dales*

IN 1948, Marie Hartley and Joan Ingilby went to their nearest post box in Askrigg, Yorkshire, and posted the manuscript of their first collaboration, *The Old Hand-Knitters of the Dales*, destined to become one of the classic social histories of knitting. Their publisher asked for only 12,000 words. Marie wrote: "In November 1948 we posted the manuscript. It was about 27,000 words, more than twice the number originally allotted to us, but we do not remember any protests."

During the final stages of writing, Marie's father died. Marie wrote with customary Yorkshire briskness: "Alas, the self-employed have need to strike a balance between duty and work." After struggling through this hard time to bring the manuscript to completion, the women had to endure publication being delayed another two years.

Miss Hartley was a personal friend of Dalesman founder and publisher Harry J. Scott, and the articles that she and Ella Pontefract had contributed had helped establish the *Dalesman* as a great magazine with a growing readership. Marie and Joan must have been confident that their book would soon be in print. In fact, it would languish on their publisher's desk for two years before finally, in June 1951, *Old Hand-Knitters of the Dales* saw the light of day.

Post-war paper shortages were partly to blame, although Dalesman published a number of other books between 1948 and 1951, even whilst conforming to "authorized economy standards." The delay for *Old Hand-Knitters* might have

Introduction to the Revised Edition

resulted from the perception that knitting was a minority interest, or "just for women." Years later, Marie said:

> In 1948 we found that very little work had been done on either knitting in general or knitting as a branch of the textile industry in the Dales and elsewhere. It was inclined to be thought of as a hobby entirely for women.

Once the book finally appeared, it stayed in print, on and off, for decades, becoming one of Dalesman's most popular titles.

Despite their success with the book, our two authors were not themselves knitters. At mid-century, hand-knitting was a fading, but once vital, part of Yorkshire's heritage, and so they felt compelled to document it.

The original manuscript of *The Old Hand-Knitters of the Dales* is lost to us. A former neighbour of the ladies confided in me that Marie and Ella were not as rigorous as they might have been when it came to documenting or keeping primary sources. This erratic record-keeping appears to have extended to the original typescript of their own book as well. I enquired after it at Dalesman, at the Yorkshire Archaeological Society where the women's notes and documents are stored, and at the Dales Countryside Museum, which Marie Hartley founded. I drew a blank everywhere.

As we were unable to work from the manuscript, this new edition is a faithful reproduction of the 1951 first edition—with some added, twenty-first century bonuses.

~

Knitters have read and loved this little book for more than sixty years, and yet have never been afforded a glimpse of its enigmatic authors. Marie Hartley was born in 1905 into a family of wool merchants in Morley, Leeds. Marie started her working life as an illustrator. All her life, she thought of herself as an artist; writing was almost incidental. Yet, her reputation as an artist was eclipsed by her success as a writer and Yorkshire historian—in collaboration first with Ella Pontefract and then with Joan Ingilby. Those who knew Marie say that she was a force of nature, taking the upper hand when dealing with publishers and public alike. Back copies of the *Dalesman* contain a number of interviews with Marie, for instance, but none directly with Joan. Marie seems to have been a formidable, admirable woman, who knew her own mind and drove her own career.

Foreword

Marie sometimes said she thought of herself primarily as an artist, yet her art was only exhibited as a body when she was in her 90s. She began her art education in 1926, attending Leeds College of Art from her home in Wetherby, and then moving on in 1931 to the prestigious Slade College of Art in London, where she became an accomplished wood engraver and illustrator. In 1992, interviewed about her life as an artist, she said, "I was formally trained to be an illustrator, not a painter."

Her first collaborator, Ella Pontefract, shared Marie's tiny London flat while Ella studied folklore at University College and Marie studied art. It was during her time working with Ella that Marie developed all the skills and interests that culminated in *Old Hand-Knitters*.

Brought up in genteel Wetherby, on the flat Vale of York—famous for its race course—Marie had developed a love for the dramatic uplands of the Yorkshire Dales during her school years in Leyburn, Wensleydale. Throughout her student years in London, she was fascinated by her memories of the Dales. In the 1930s, Marie and Ella joined one of Marie's cousins and a friend on a number of walking tours of the Dales. It was during one of these that Marie and Ella decided to document the countryside and its rapidly changing way of life. They would borrow their family's cars—an Austin 7 and an old Alvis; and for the earliest book, they stayed in a caravan, parking it at Redmire, amongst other places. In an interview decades later, Marie said of writing about the Dales: "It was an open book, to us—and no-one else was writing it." Marie and Ella are said to have returned from the Dales "with bulging notebooks and a car laden with domestic and agricultural paraphernalia". ['Voice of the Dales', Terry Fletcher, *Dalesman*, July 2006].

Marie and Ella collaborated on six books, mainly for the London publishers J. M. Dent & Sons. Marie had been given a letter of introduction to the publishing house; Dent were known for producing books with well-crafted engravings.

Later in the process of putting together *Old Hand-Knitters*, Marie and Ella saw and fell in love with a dilapidated seventeenth-century house called Coleshouse. In 1941, Marie bought it and moved in. She painted, sketched and made engravings "between books."

In the early days, the collaborative books came out under the names of "Ella Pontefract & Marie Hartley"—Ella's top billing implying that she was the writer and Marie the illustrator. Marie was to say later: "You know, when

Introduction to the Revised Edition

Ella and I started, I started as the artist and Ella as the writer." Ella's prose style was elegant, well-researched, and managed to be both romantic and unsentimental at the same time.

Their early books for Dent included *Swaledale*, *Wensleydale*, *Wharfedale*, and *Yorkshire Tour*. One title, *The Charm of Yorkshire Churches*, was published by the well-respected Leeds newspaper, *The Yorkshire Post*.

Their 1942 book, *Yorkshire Cottage*, told the story of their acquisition and restoration of Coleshouse, in Askrigg. Marie's illustrations were masterly, conveying the moods of the mutable Dales landscape and the character of Dalesfolk they met on their adventure. Some of the Dales folk described in the book seem like precursors to James Herriot's characters—perhaps not that surprising since both the real and fictional characters hail from the same time and place. Tourism barely existed in the Dales in the '30s, although that began to burgeon after the publication of the women's earliest books, *Swaledale* and *Wensleydale*; the tourist industry accelerated even further in the 1970s after the publication of Herriot's *All Creatures Great and Small* series.

Ella's writing style in that final collaboration is delicate and elegiac. Had she lived, *Old Hand-Knitters* would have been a very different book. Ella died unexpectedly in 1945 of chronic high blood pressure, leaving Marie to cope with both emotional and professional grief. Marie may initially have had some difficulty persuading her publisher to stick with her after Ella's death, as Ella was perceived to be "the writer." One thing is certain: there was a long gap between Marie's last book with Ella in 1942 and her first with Joan Ingilby in 1951.[1] That nine-year hiatus was the longest of Marie's career. In short, *Old Hand-Knitters* was a milestone: a return to form, a personal triumph, and above all a professional success. It was a testament to Marie's determination that she continued with the book she had then under contract, insisting that she had been a writer, too, and could carry the work forward.

∼

---

1   Ella and Marie had been writing a book about every 18 months to two years, and the one book Marie that published alone, a tribute to Ella, was actually written after *Old Hand-Knitters* (although it was published earlier, in 1950). Marie went on to publish at least 25 books after Ella's death, most of them with Joan.

Foreword

Marie was not a knitter, but she was an artist and appreciated other folk's handwork as an art form. Ever modest, Marie once told an interviewer: "I can draw well—not as well as David Hockney but pretty well, I think." Marie's method as an artist was rapidly to sketch a pencil drawing from life, and then later transform the drawing into a wood engraving. She believed that the sheer craftsmanship involved in creating the wood engravings gave the books their atmosphere of romance.

As an artist, Marie Hartley deserves to be in the company of the many stellar artists who came out of the Slade in the early twentieth century: artists like Mark Gertler, Paul Nash, and Stanley Spencer. That is her context. Marie counted Yorkshire literary giants J. B. Priestley and Phyllis Bentley amongst her friends. Although her subject matter was regional, she transcended the parochial and as a recorder of social history, was nationally recognised.

The Old Hand-Knitters of the Dales illustrations are no less technically competent than earlier work; but somehow lack the human interest and fine detail of the art for its predecessor, *Yorkshire Cottage*. Something fragile and indefinable left with Ella. Yet *Old Hand-Knitters'* illustrations have a romance of their own.

~

Many more recent readers of *The Old Hand-Knitters of the Dales* would have no reason to know that it was the first book Marie wrote after Ella's death, and with her new writing partner, Joan Ingilby. It was also the first book for a new publisher, Dalesman.

We don't know whether Marie and Ella had already planned *Old Hand-Knitters* together, or whether Marie hatched the idea for the book after her friend's sudden death. Either way, she seems to have been working on it by 1947, the year that her old friend Joan moved in at Coleshouse.

Joan remains a bit of a mystery: in the numerous interviews that the women gave to *Dalesman* magazine from the 1950s–90s, Marie was always the spokesperson; Joan stayed in the shadows. In one lengthy interview, when both women were questioned, Joan barely spoke at all.

Joan was born in 1911 in North Stainley, near Ripon, and moved to Coleshouse in the infamous, brutally cold winter of 1947. Before her partnership with Marie, she was already a published writer and had been amongst the group of friends who went on walking holidays with Marie and Ella in the pre-war

Introduction to the Revised Edition

years. Her writing style was perhaps more workmanlike than Ella's, but her grasp of detail was impressive.

Marie once described how the women worked together. They sat at opposite ends of their work room and wrote alternate chapters of their books. After visiting them, newspaper editor Malcolm Barker commented: "They write as one." Their work was seamless. Marie had the eye for detail; while Joan provided the overall, cohesive vision. Each edited the other's chapters, and both put their stamp on every word. They would travel, take extensive notes in longhand, and Marie would sketch, then return to Coleshouse to write. Sometimes they borrowed sources, such as old mill records. Sometimes they were just shown the records and had to make hasty notes on the spot.

Between 1934 and 1998, Marie wrote a vast body of work on Yorkshire life, lore, and history. In 1950, when *Old Hand-Knitters* was still sitting patiently on their publisher's desk, Marie brought out a rare solo work: *Yorkshire Heritage, A Memoir to Ella Pontefract*. Presumably this was written during the hiatus between writing *Old Hand-Knitters* and its publication. Marie based her tribute on diaries kept during their time at Coleshouse. It is interesting to speculate how Joan may have felt as Marie wrote the memoir.

After *Old Hand-Knitters* was published, Marie continued to collaborate with Joan. For many, their work culminated in 1968 with *Life and Traditions in the Yorkshire Dales*. The women amassed a vast archive of research material during their travels around the Dales, and all of their books would emerge from this morass of notes. Marie once said that of the more than 30 books she had written and co-written, her favorite was *Yorkshire Village*, their book about their home village, Askrigg in Wensleydale. Certainly, she is still fondly remembered in the village.

During the writing of *Old Hand-Knitters*, Marie attended auctions, rescuing old farm artifacts and vital pieces of domestic history, such as knitting sticks, from being sold out of the county. Later, locals heard the women had "a sort of museum" at Coleshouse, and donated material.

The women wrote together in a room full of books and papers, and the rest of their house, over the years, became increasingly overwhelmed by Marie's accidental museum. The collection of rural paraphernalia eventually formed the core of the Upper Dales Folk Museum, which Marie opened in 1979 in Hawes. This is now the Dales Countryside Museum and houses the knitting

Foreword

sticks, Dales gloves, stockings, and other artifacts that Marie and Joan discuss in *Old Hand-Knitters*.

The museum was Marie's proudest achievement. In 1983, she told an interviewer she wished they "had recorded on cinefilm some of the local traditions and pastimes, for example the old hand knitting." On another occasion she said:

> The swift execution in knitting was achieved by the exponent being taught as a child, often by her father. We wish that we had borrowed a cine camera and recorded Mrs Crabtree in action, for this skill is something which has gone, never to be seen again in the Yorkshire Dales.

There is no known film in existence of the super-fast Yorkshire method of knitting called *swaving*, and people still speculate how it might have been done. Marie and Joan succeeded in pulling back for us much of what might have been lost and for that, generations of knitters will be grateful to these two non-knitters.

~

Asked in 1981 about the writing of *Old Hand-Knitters*, Marie remarked on the changes in the Dales during her lifetime:

> Even then we were told 'Oh, what a change! What a change!' by Mr William Gill, aged 89, when we talked to him. His father and his two brothers had the woollen mill, Low Mill, at Askrigg, and they used to take the 'rove' yarn (white wool) to Hurst and Marrick in Swaledale ... When offering the steel needles to the knitters, they asked: 'Do you want straight or crooked?' The true Dales knitters worked on curved needles... Their earnings 6d or 7d for knitting a pair of stockings—was a pittance, but clothes were very cheap (30s for a suit)....
>
> Many talks were remembered of Molly Kirkbride, a famous knitter long since dead. She once heard Elijah Allen of Hawes telephoning to Leeds, and was dumbfounded at this marvel and remarked to excuse her ignorance: 'We were nobbut brought up like bullocks.' ...
>
> A friend in Swaledale was Mrs David Harker of Muker.... She gave us a top crook, made out of a Georgian penny... The design of the top crook exactly parallels the cowband with which cows were formerly tethered to the stall, the difference being the top crook was made of

Introduction to the Revised Edition

> metal and quite small whereas the cowband was large and made of wood....
>
> Another walk led us to Ravenstonedale along a farm track three miles ... where we had heard there was a spinning gallery. Although we have never been since, no doubt it is still there.

The famous illustrations of the Ravenstonedale spinning gallery were, no doubt, completed that day.

As the above quotes indicate, instead of spending all of their time rifling through library archives, Marie and Joan were constantly out and about in the Dales, actively collecting items, talking to local people, and building their unique data bank of information about the social history of the Dales.

Considering that Marie and Joan had no internet, cars that overheated alarmingly on hills, and sporadic public transport up in the Dales in the late 1940s, we shouldn't underestimate the sheer legwork that went into the book's research. The women walked and talked with locals, tirelessly and in all weathers, returning to their work room in the Askrigg cottage to write up the day's findings. When asked to name her favorite aspect of researching the book, Marie answered:

> Possibly a walk to Hebblethwaite Hall, two miles North East of Sedbergh, gave us our greatest thrill ... we had been lent a ledger from this mill.... One letter, written in February 1822, reported: 'It is only a few of the old knitters ... that can now manage all sorts of caps and these are not good to meet with.' Even then the traditional skills were disappearing. Mr and Mrs Bentham have since died and we have been unable to trace the present whereabouts of the fascinating ledger.

I have looked for this ledger, and have also failed to determine its whereabouts. If these women hadn't written this book when they did, so much would have been lost to today's knitters and historians.

> We found and saw one person knitting in the old way, Mrs Crabtree of Flintergill, Dent, then in her 79th year. We were told to go and see her, and when we knocked at her door she opened it with her knitting in her hand and a knitting sheath tucked in her apron band....
>
> We regret that we did not meet her sister, Polly Stephenson, who also used the 'swaving' action in knitting.

Foreword

Marie received an honorary degree at the University of Leeds in 1968. Later, Marie and Joan were awarded honorary degrees from the University of York and the Open University. In 1993 the Yorkshire Archaeological Society awarded the two women medals for their contribution to Yorkshire history, and in 1997 the women were made Members of the Most Excellent Order of the British Empire (M.B.E.) for services to the culture and history of Yorkshire. Joan died in 2000, aged 89.

Both women were pioneers of social history, keepers of Yorkshire lore, and restored to us invaluable knitting history that otherwise would have been lost forever. In the *Yorkshire Journal*, Malcolm Barker wrote of Marie and Joan: "They are unchallenged in their grasp of Yorkshire tradition, overshadowing all others."

Marie died in 2006, in her 101st year. Writer Terry Fletcher said of Marie: "My last memory of her was meeting her at an exhibition of her work in Hawes and offering her a lift home. Then in her mid-nineties, she politely declined, saying she had driven herself."

—*Penelope Lister Hemingway, York, 2013*

Thanks go to: Thelma Bannister; Jeff Cowton, M.B.E., curator, The Wordsworth Trust's Museum, Grasmere; the Yorkshire Archaeological Society, Leeds; the Dales Countryside Museum, Hawes; Swaledale Museum, Reeth; York City Reference Library; and Leeds City Reference Library.

Introduction to the Revised Edition

BIBLIOGRAPHY TO THE FOREWORD

Barker, Malcolm. "Wonders of Yorkshire: The Life and Works of Marie Hartley and Joan Ingilby." *The Yorkshire Journal*. Spring, 1996.

Fletcher, Terry. "Voice of the Dales." *Dalesman*, Vol 68. July, 2006.

Kinder, Kathleen. "Knitting in the Dales Way." *Dalesman*, Vol 42. February 1981.

Hartley, Marie, and Joan Ingilby. "Quest for the Hand-Knitters." *Dalesman*. August 1970.

Interview with Marie Hartley and Joan Ingilby, William Mitchell's archive, PDF document: www.wrmitchellarchive.org.uk

Morgan-Rees, David. "Heritage of Patience." *Yorkshire Life*, Vol. 37. February 1983.

Morgan-Rees, David. "Marie Hartley: A Distinguished Yorkshire Artist-Writer in a New Light." *Dalesman*, Vol. 54. November 1992.

Pontefract, Ella, and Marie Hartley. *Yorkshire Cottage*. London: J.M.Dent & Sons, 1942.

The Terrible Knitters E' Dent

The OLD HAND-KNITTERS of the DALES

With an Introduction to
THE EARLY HISTORY OF KNITTING

by

MARIE HARTLEY

and

JOAN INGILBY

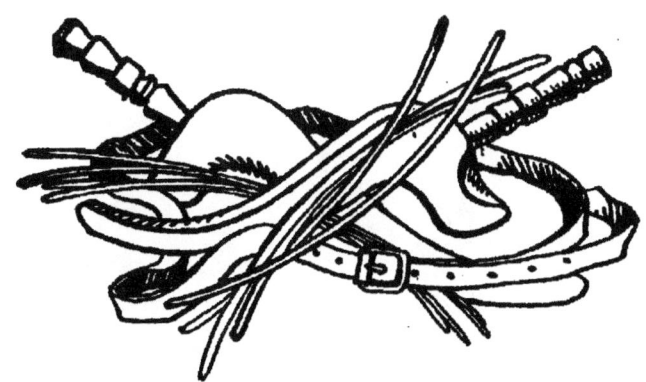

Originally published in 1951

ORIGINAL FOREWORD

WHEN the Editor of *The Dalesman* suggested that we should write a pamphlet on the hand-knitting industry in the Yorkshire and Westmorland Dales, we anticipated that little information would be forthcoming. But instead, a book has been the result of a particularly interesting piece of research work.

We wish to thank Mrs. G. Crowfoot for her advice on early textiles, Mr. R. J. Charleston for his helpful suggestions and the loan of books, Mr. J.D. Betham for allowing us to publish the contents of the *Dover Ledger* and for his enthusiastic co-operation, Mr. M. Clarkson for lending us the *Clarkson Account Book*. For their generous assistance, we thank the keepers of the following museums: Victoria and Albert Museum, Department of Textiles; The London Museum; The National Museum of Antiquities of Scotland; Bankfield Museum, Halifax; Keighley Museum; Castle Museum, York; Scarborough Museum; Wordsworth Museum, Grasmere; and The Museum of Industrial Arts, Oslo; and the librarians at The London Library, Leeds Reference Library, The Yorkshire Archaeological Society, and The County Library, Northallerton.

Lastly we thank our friends in the dales who have loaned us photographs, deeds of property, and knitting sheaths and have helped in every possible way.

M.H. J.I.

CHAPTER I
KNITTING IN EARLY TIMES

AT the present day it is unusual to find a subject, however obscure, that has not been minutely studied and the known facts recorded in a reliable standard book. But turn to 'knitting' in the Subject Index of any library, and the chances are that only references to women's magazines will be found. These include many knitting patterns, but seldom a word on the history of the craft. Encyclopedias contain meagre information. The *Oxford English Dictionary* gives many interesting references but none of an early date, and derives the word 'knit' from the Anglo-Saxon *cnittan* though this is not necessarily referring to the craft but to the verb in its general sense.

William Felkin, who in his early years was engaged in the hosiery trade and later in lace manufacture, gave evidence before a Parliamentary Commission on the state of the framework knitters; and in two papers published in 1845 he begins his survey with a brief history of knitting. In 1867 he published his book *The History of Machine-Wrought Hosiery and Lace Manufacture* which starts with a chapter on hand-knitting. This has been referred to by most later writers. *The Dictionary of Needlework* by Caulfeild and Saward (1882) gives a certain amount of facts and traditions known and believed at that date. A recent collection of facts is to be found in Mary Thomas's *Knitting and Pattern Books*. These give an exhaustive account of innumerable fancy stitches, and include photographs and descriptions of a few garments of historical interest to illustrate the development of various patterns at different periods.

The origin of knitting is still obscure. Down the ages it has been of secondary importance to weaving, seldom mentioned, few examples preserved; so that there is much room for research before the full story can be told. In this small book only a summary can be made of this general aspect in order to leave space for a detailed account of the hand-knitting industry as it affected the Yorkshire and Westmorland Dales.

The everyday life of early civilisations is pieced together from specimens of implements, pottery, textiles, and so forth, found at burial sites in many parts of the world. Spindle whorls and clay loom weights establish the antiquity of spinning and weaving, and date it as far back as the Stone Age, and in England to the Beaker people of the Bronze Age. But finds of bone pins do not prove that prehistoric peoples knitted as these could have been used for a multitude of purposes. A wealth of early textiles comes from the Dynastic periods of Egypt; and in Denmark whole garments of cloth have been found in oak coffin graves of the Early Bronze Age, 3000 B.C. In the future archaeologists may make new discoveries, but no knitted fabric has been found amongst prehistoric textiles up to date.

The earliest techniques used for a stretchable material were 'sprang' or braiding, a method by which a fabric could be woven loosely to form a sort of network or closely to make narrow material for girdles and stockings. Braiding was practiced in Egypt where it is known as 'Egyptian plait technique,' in Denmark in the Bronze Age[1]; and it is found in the vestments of St. Cuthbert, A.D. 905–16.[2] The fabric resembles knitting in that it has a right and a wrong side. Netting, known in the Stone Age, is related to knitting in that one continuous thread is used; and an important form of it is coiling or half-knot work employed by primitive peoples for an elastic fabric. This technique has many variations. One, for example, is the Swedish Vantsöm used for mittens which were found at Västergötland. They date from the early centuries of the Christian era.[3] But although these techniques have some affinity with our subject they are not knitting.

The earliest known pieces of knitting to which a definite date can be affixed belong to the third century. Three fragments come from the Syrian city of Dura which fell about 256 A.D.[4], and a tiny knitted cap in fawn wool is from Coptic burial grounds at Bahnasâ, Egypt. Of the three fragments, two have bands of colour, and the third of undyed wool is knitted in an elaborate stitch. The cap is preserved at the Victoria and Albert Museum together with other Coptic knitted articles, such as a pair of red socks with divided toes, a blue

---

1   *The Costumes of the Bronze Age in Denmark.* H. C. Broholm and Margrethe Hald.

2   *The Tablet-woven Braids from the Vestments of St. Cuthbert at Durham.* Grace M. Crowfoot.

3   *Ciba Review No. 63. Basic Textile Techniques.*

4   *The Excavations at Dura-Europos.* Part II *The Textiles.* R. Pfister and Louisa Bellinger. (This book gives the complete knitting pattern of the third fragment).

wool sock, a green and yellow bag, and a child's sock striped red and yellow, all of which date from the fourth and fifth centuries. It is fascinating to see these ancient knitted articles, the socks in particular, apart from the division for the big toe, might be modern ankle socks; and the colours are excellent. One sock is patched with little squares of knitting. The technique is not quite our modern method, but is Crossed Eastern Stitch, in which for the knit stitch the needle is inserted into the back of the loop, and the same for the purl. In ancient times knitting needles were hooked; and Mary Thomas describes some left in a half-finished sock found in a twelfth-century Turkish tomb.

Other early knitting is Peruvian from the Early Nazca period which corresponds with the time of the Coptic garments at the beginnings of Christianity. It is particularly elaborate and takes on a special form of three-dimensional knitting.[5] The art of knitting appears to have spread from Syria and Egypt, and probably carried by Arab traders and the Moors, reached Spain and France. A knitting industry developed in France; and the hand-knitters formed a guild in 1527 with St. Fiacre as their Patron Saint.

How early it became known in England we cannot be sure. The first mention may be in 1320, when two pairs of 'caligae de Wyrstede' (gaskins or gaiters) at 11½d. are listed in an Oxford inventory. These are given in *A History of Agriculture and Prices in England* by Thorold Rogers who states that they seem to be knitted goods. At that time worsted cloths were largely used for leg-coverings, but they had usually specific names, so that this evidence is perhaps correct, but is not conclusive.

In Scandinavia, so far as is known at present, knitting was not practiced until the seventeenth century; and the earliest knitted garments preserved in Norway are six silk shirts which are described later. In some of the dales of Norway and Sweden there are still remnants of braided works ('sprang') which was bound in strips round the legs prior to knitted stockings; and in these remote districts knitting is still called 'binding.' In considering Scandinavia we think of patterns—a study in themselves. Variations in knitting can be obtained by fancy stitches or by the use of many colours. Of the former, fishermen's jerseys are an example of a long tradition in the craft. Of the latter, specimens from the fourteenth and fifteenth centuries in Egypt show coloured designs which resemble the well-known Fair Isles ones.[6] In

---

5   *Textile Periods in Ancient Peru.* Lila M. O'Neale and A. L. Kroeber. (Pointed out to us by Mr. J. Norbury).

6   *Cotton in Medieval Textiles of the Near East.* Carl Johan Lamm. 1937.

fact patterns in the Faroes, Fair Isle, Scandinavia, Russia, and Jugo-Slavia all bear a certain resemblance to one another. Jugo-Slavia in modern times can produce knitted boots in which 'the use of colour, interest of design, and sheer ingenuity of craftsmanship' have never been surpassed.[7]

Of medieval knitting we have preserved at New College, Oxford, a pair of crimson silk knitted gloves, probably Spanish. They are the gloves of the Founder, William of Wykeham, Bishop of Winchester, and were worn by him at the opening ceremony of the college in 1386. Knitted in fine stocking stitch, they have bands of gold thread at the base of the fingers and thumbs, a radiating design with I.H.S. on the back of each hand, and patterned cuffs with green octofoils.[8]

Similar in character but of a later date the vestments of a bishop were discovered in 1855 when a tomb was opened in the ruined Cathedral Church of Fortrose in the Highlands of Scotland. A small piece of yellow khaki-coloured knitting is preserved at the National Museum of Antiquities of Scotland. This is considered by the museum authorities to be from a silk knitted glove, part of the vestments of Bishop Cairnross, who died not earlier than 1545 and who was buried at Fortrose. It is of special interest because in the description of the finding of the garments the legs were clothed in long silk stockings similar in appearance to the gloves.[9] These like the gloves at New College would no doubt be of French or Spanish origin, and they are the earliest record that we have found of tangible evidence of silk stockings in the British Isles.

In 1488 a will in the Ripon Chapter Acts mentions a 'knit gyrdyll.' We know that Edward IV had knitted garments in his wardrobe, and that Princess Mary, sister of Henry VIII, was provided with two pairs of knit hose. Then Stow says that Henry VIII 'did wear only cloth hose or cut out of ell broad taffety, or that by a great chance there came a pair of Spanish silke stockings from Spaine.' An inventory of Henry VIII's wardrobe mentions 'one pair of hose of white silk and gold knit, bought of Christopher Milloner.' In 1553 the household book of Sir Thomas L'Estrange of Hunstanton, Norfolk, records the payment of 8/- for a pair of knit hose, and 1/- for two pair of the same for the children.[10]

---

7 *Essays on National Art in Yugo-Slavia.* 1944.
8 see *Archaeologia* Vol. 60. Part 2.
9 *Proceedings of the Society of Antiquarians of Scotland.* Vol. 1. 1855.
10 *Preface to Progresses of Queen Elizabeth.* J. Nichols (1823).

Knitting in Early Times

Next came the historic occasion, quoted by innumerable writers from Howell's *History of the World*, when in 1561 Mrs. Montague, the Queen's silkwoman, presented Her Majesty with a pair of black silk stockings, and 'thenceforth she never wore cloth hose any more.' This is not confirmed by the list of New Year's gifts given to the Queen in 1561 printed in *The Progresses of Queen Elizabeth* by J. Nichols, (1823). But in that year she received several pairs of 'silk knytt hoose,' besides other knitted garments; and in 1588 Mrs. Vaughan gave her 'a pair of silk stockings.' It was also fashionable to give the Queen silk purses containing gold coins. In 1561 as many as twenty-eight of these were knitted. One of them presented by the Duke of Norfolk was of purple silk and gold. A pair of yellow stockings supposed to have been worn by the Queen is preserved at Hatfield House.

In this and the next century knitting reached a height of superb craftsmanship. Three seventeenth-century Italian garments at the Victoria and Albert Museum are in fine coloured silks—two include gold thread—and are knitted in floral and brocade designs. The London Museum has a vest which belonged to Charles I. It is of blue silk and knitted in a fancy stitch. The Bergen Museum possesses one and the Kunstindustrimuseet, Oslo, three magnificent seventeenth-century women's silk shirts which are knitted in an all-over pattern of diagonal checks and stars in stocking and purl stitch. On this background elaborate floral designs are embroidered in coloured silks.

This then is an outline of the story of early knitting. Its organisation and development as an industry in the British Isles will be shown in the next chapter.

Richmond

CHAPTER II
THE KNITTING INDUSTRY

THE industry of hand-knitted clothing has in this country a historical record of over four hundred years. It cannot compare in importance with the cloth trade, and was almost from its beginnings overshadowed by machines for knitting. But in spite of diminishing fortunes it provided a livelihood through the centuries for thousands of people mostly women and children, but often men, who otherwise would have been in desperate straits; and of the garments made, stockings undoubtedly took first place.

Hose in the magnificent fashions of the Gothic period were made of cloth and all in one piece from waist to foot. They may have sometimes been knitted, and women in medieval days may have worn knitted leg-coverings under their long dresses; but we have no proof. In one of the Paston Letters, dated

Old Hand-Knitters of the Dales

September 1465, there is a charming appeal to his mother by Young John. He asks her to see that the black and russet hose 'be ready for use at the hosier's with the crooked back,' and continues, 'I beseech you that the gear be not forgotten, for I have not an whole hose for to don.' Whether these hose were knitted or not is a matter for conjecture.

In the next century about 1510 there occurred a change in fashion of supreme importance to hand-knitting. Men's hose were divided into two and became upper and nether stocks, from which we get our name stocking; and eventually the term hose became synonymous with stocking as it has remained ever since. An early mention of knitted hose was in 1519 when a pair cost 5d. at Nottingham.[1] These were, in all probability, coarse worsted, whilst as we have seen, royalty and the nobility were beginning to wear elaborate and expensive silk knitted stockings.

All types of leg-coverings from this transitional period are given amongst the goods of a tradesman, James Backhouse of Kirkby Lonsdale, Lancashire. His inventory taken in 1578 includes: hose, women's hose, nether stocks, and men's stockings.[2] Stubbes in his *Anatomie of Abuses* 1596 writes:

> 'Then have they neather stocks to these gay hosen, not of cloth (though never so fine), for that is thought too base, but of jarnsey, worsted, crewell, silke, thread, and such like, or else, at the least, of the finest yarn that can be got; and so curiously knitte with open seame doune the legge, with quirkes and clocks about the ancles, and sometyme (haplie) interlaced about the ancles with gold or silver threads as is wonderful to beholde. And to such impudent insolency and shameful outrage it is now growne, that everyone almost though otherwise very poor, having scarce forty shillings wages by the year, will not stick to have two or three pair of these silk nether stocks, or else of the finest yarn that may be got, though the price of them be a royal, or twenty shillings, or more, as commonly it is; for how can they be lesse, when as the very knitting of them is worth a noble or a royal, and some much more? The time hath been when one might have clothed all his body well, from top to toe, for lesse than a pair of these nether stockes will cost.[3]

---

1   *Victoria County History Nottingham*. Vol. 2. p352.
2   *Wills and Inventories, Archdeaconry of Richmond*. Surtees Soc. Vol. 26.
3   See Fairholt—*Costume in England*.

The Knitting Industry

Caps, however, were knitted in the fifteenth century. An Act of Parliament in 1488 stated that the price of knitted woollen caps was 2s. 8d.; and in fact several Acts mention 'knitte cappes' in the ensuing years. Here then is the first record of knitted goods manufactured for sale in England. To encourage the trade, as well as knitting as an employment, an Act of 1571 reads, 'Every person not possessed of 20 marks rental should wear on Sundays and Holy Days when not on travell, a woollen knit cap, on pain of forfeiting 3s. 4d. a day.'

These caps were the flat type commonly worn in Tudor times, and two in the London Museum are knitted and felted to a rainproof material. Felting, comparable with the fulling of cloth, is an ancient method of shrinking and matting together a woollen fabric by soaking it in hot water.

These caps were similar to the Scottish bonnet supposedly imported from France into the Lowlands in the sixteenth century, and, in time, so commonly worn that 'Blue Caps' became a term of ridicule given to the Scots. There is an old ballad 'Blue Cap for me.' From Elizabethan times Kilmarnock became a centre for the manufacture of these knitted caps, and in 1646 had about thirty makers.[4] The trade continued without a break, and to this day is carried on by the firm of J. L. Currie and Company which makes Glengarries and Balmorals for Scottish regiments. But since 1870 they have been knitted on machines invented by the owner of the firm. Kilmarnock caps enter into our story again in close connection with the knitting industry in Yorkshire.

Then, in 1589, occurred an event which only reached its full climax during the last century. It was in the year after England had celebrated the defeat of the Armada, that an obscure curate, named William Lee, of Nottinghamshire invented the first stocking-loom. The Queen, herself, saw it work, but was disappointed to find that it only produced worsted hose. She refused Lee a patent monopoly, and said, 'I have too much love for my poor people who obtain their bread by the employment of knitting, to give my money to forward an invention that will tend to their ruin.' And 'If Mr. Lee make a machine that would have made silk stockings, I should, I think, have been somewhat justified in granting him a patent for that monopoly.' Not to be daunted by the Queen's requirements, by 1598 Lee and his brother had devised a machine capable of making silk hose, but Elizabeth still refused to give him either a patent or money. After the Queen's death hope revived, but James I took no interest. Lee, in the end, went first to Paris where he was unlucky, and lastly to Rouen where he died. His brother returned to London with

---

4   Mackay's *History of Kilmarnock*.

the frames, and sold them—thus establishing the trade in the south. He, then, went to Nottingham, and with a new partner constructed others with important improvements.[5]

The invention was to have little effect on ordinary knitting for very many years. The expansion of the trade in garments hand-knitted by people in their homes still continued. An Act of Parliament of Edward VI, 1552, had mentioned 'Knitte hose, knitte petticoats, knitte gloves, knitte sleeves.' In Elizabeth's reign the production of worsted stockings was encouraged by the Queen as a branch of the wool trade, and it became an integral part of the economic life of the nation. Her reign marks the beginning of a state organisation for poor relief; and knitting, amongst other crafts, was taught to provide work.

A handicraft that aimed to produce quantities of goods had to reach a high degree of efficiency and skill, so that knitting schools were started in towns up and down the country. At Lincoln, one begun in 1591 continued throughout the next century.[6] In 1590 the York burgesses took a house in St. Saviourgate where poor children under three teachers were taught to knit. A clause in the municipal records reads: 'That such poore children at the Knitting Scole as stand in need of Coots—shall have coots of the cheapest graye that can be gotten.'[7] (One wishes that the promoters of this charitable institution did not sound quite so niggardly.) Four years later the head of the school was reprimanded for neglecting to take apprentices so that there was a danger of the trade dying out. We believe that the rhythmic fast method of knitting employed up to this century in the North of England and Scotland—and still practiced in the Shetland Islands—was the one taught. The project did not apparently succeed in York where there was a choice of many trades. As we shall see it was in the country districts with limited resources that hand-knitting flourished.

In Elizabeth's reign came the first beginnings of the changeover from the medieval distaff to the spinning-wheel. The production of yarn in sufficient quantities was always a stumbling-block in the woollen trade; but a spinner, at any rate in later years, could supply yarn sufficient to keep four or five knitters in constant work. Spinning and knitting were both domestic occupations

---

5   See *Machine-Wrought Hosiery and Lace Manufacture*. William Felkin.

6   *The Economic History of England*. Vol. III. E. Lipson.

7   *Victoria County History of Yorkshire*. Vol. 2, p. 413.

The Knitting Industry

undertaken by the women and children who sat working at cottage doors, as indeed they may still be seen in isolated parts of Europe. The latter half of the sixteenth century witnessed a tide of emigration of Dutchmen and Walloons who fleeing from Spanish tyranny and religious persecution came to England and settled chiefly round Norwich. They excelled in the art of weaving, and improved the quality of the stuff already made in England and brought 'New Draperies'. In a manuscript, dated 1592, we find a list of these goods amongst which are two sorts of knit stockings which bore a very high rate of duty levied.

'Knytt Hose, short storks, the dozen pair
5lbs, valued at (the pair) 0 – 4 – 0
poize (weight)

Knytt Hose, long storks, the dozen pair
6lbs, valued at (the pair) 0 – 5 – 0
poize.'[8]

The 'New Draperies' were not by any means all new, but were often variations of the old ones; and in the case of stockings may have been a special type. They appear again in a comprehensive survey of the knitting trade at Richmond, Yorkshire at the same date.

In 1605 James I granted the aulnage of 'New Draperies' to the Duke of Lennox.[9] The aulnager to whom the office was farmed out inspected the goods for quality, affixed seals, and enforced the payment of duty. Amongst these draperies were 'knitt-hose of worsted, knitt wast coates, knitt sleeves, knitt gloves, knitt cappes, knitt coyfes, knitt hatts, knitt socks'. The 'knit coyfes' remind us of the Elizabethan clouts, napkins or kerchiefs, worn by country-women described by Thynne in *The debate between pride and lowliness*.

'With homely clouts y-knit upon their head,
Simple, yet white as they so coarse might be.'

By this time the hand-knitting had settled in different centres: in Norwich where the output had a weekly value of five to ten thousand shillings,[10] in Dorset and Hampshire, Leicestershire, Nottinghamshire, Yorkshire, and in Scotland. In 1689 on one of her journeys through England, Celia Fiennes

---

8   *History of the Worsted Manufacture.* J. James. p. 126.
9   Pat. 3 Jas I pt XVII 6 Oct 1605.
10 *Women Workers and the Industrial Revolution.* Ivy Pinchbeck.

paused at Gloucester, and noted in her diary: 'here they follow knitting, stockings gloves wastcoates peticoates and sleeves all of cotten, and others spin the cottens.'

Meanwhile the knitting-frames invented by Lee were being made in increasing numbers; and during the Commonwealth the frame-work knitters petitioned Cromwell for a charter 'like other London trades.' A clause in the petition reads, 'Their trade is properly stiled frame-work knitting because it is direct or absolute knitwork in the stitches thereof, nothing different from the common way of knitting (not much more anciently for public use practiced in this nation than this).' This charter was enrolled in the City archives in July, 1657; and later under Charles II a new one was obtained. To this day the Worshipful Company of Framework Knitters is closely associated with the great machine-wrought hosiery industry. But the whole fascinating story is too long to be told here—of the Master Stockiners, apprenticeship, Luddite Riots, and all the improvements to machines up to the most modern types in use today, capable of making considerably more than a million loops a minute, and of producing fine silk hose.[11]

Hand-knitting and frame-work knitting continued side by side as separate industries throughout the seventeenth century. Because of the widely dispersed centres and the fact that the workers were mostly women, the hand-knitters never aspired to a guild as did the frame-work knitters or the knitters of Paris who, as already stated, formed a guild in 1527. But indirectly through other trades such as the cappers the guilds had some control. Under the 'domestic system' it flourished, on a small scale, in the same way as the cloth trade and the yeomen-clothiers rose to their zenith before the Industrial Revolution.

The uneasy companionship continued until the last half of the eighteenth century. Then the black storm that had been hovering over the hand-knitting industry broke as the machine-produced garments by sheer weight of numbers began to effect their rivals. Fine stockings became almost exclusively machine-made, so leaving only the coarser work to be hand-knitted. The latter industry was driven from centres in towns such as Norwich, which had for example in 1724 almost lost its trade,[12] but it established itself more firmly than ever in isolated country districts. In the Shetland Isles where knitting was, for the crofters, the most important industry as it is today, stockings

---

11   *British Knitwear and Hosiery*. S. G. Mason.
12   Defoe. *Tour through England and Wales.*

The Knitting Industry

were made from fine wool worth a guinea to twenty-five shillings a pair, and in 1800 it was estimated that stockings were exported in a year to the value of £17,000.[13] In Wales at Bala 'great markets' were held 'every Saturday morning, when from two to five hundred pounds' worth of woollen goods were sold each week (1781).'[14] Welsh hosiers then valued the annual sale at £17,000 to £19,000. While the yearly export from Aberdeen was in 1805 estimated at £100,000. The trade in Dorset and Hampshire, once much larger, had in 1793 at Wimborne and 1799 at Christchurch each a thousand knitters. And we must not omit the area of our own survey where at Kendal in 1770 stockings were the chief manufacture employing 5,000 workers including woolcombers, spinners, and knitters.[15] Wages for knitting had become miserably low, in Scotland as little as twopence a day, and in Wales a shilling a week, yet knitting was a vital and often the only means of earning a living if a meagre one in remote districts.

The eighteenth century was a time of change, of progress in social reform and mechanical invention. In education Charity Schools were founded in large numbers—a typical clause in the regulations reads: 'Children shall wear their caps, bands, clothes and other marks of distinction, every day; and that the mistresses should teach the girls to read, knit, sew and other things requisite to their sex.' Odious though the compulsory wearing of distinctive clothing was, knitted charity caps as we shall see were made by the hosiery manufactures for sale.

It was an age of enclosurers, of improved methods of farming, and of the last flowering of the yeomen and statesmen. An age when travel and communication had never been easier owing to the building of turnpike roads and canals. Yet highwaymen and footpads might be lying in wait ready to attack the traveller at cross-roads or lonely passes.

The invention of the steam-engine started a train of events closely connected with our story; for eventually the stocking-frames were run by steam-power. Until the latter part of the century yarn was spun in the homes, and in remote

---

13 *The Historical Geography of the Shetland Isles.* Andrew O'Dell, 1939.
14 *Pennant's Tour in Wales.*
15 Arthur Young's *Tour to the North.*

parts the spinning-wheel continued well into the next century. Wordsworth writes in 'Michael,' (1800):

'while far into the night
The housewife plied her own peculiar work,
Making the cottage through the silent hours
Murmur as with the sound of summer flies.'

By 1780–90, in districts far from the scenes of their origin, carding-engines began to lighten the work of the hand-carder and the wool-comber, and Hargreave's Spinning Jenny was installed in mills built by river and beck. Families often had a long tradition in the trade, and the hosier became the mill-owner, a hosiery manufacturer still employing hand-knitters.

The Industrial Revolution was at hand; and its approach spelled the end of the country crafts. Hand-knitting, fore-doomed two centuries ago by Lee's invention, struggled on unable to compete with knitting machines in producing enough goods for the market. Revivals occurred here and there: for example in Donegal in 1887 it was reorganised to relieve the poverty of the people. In the Shetland Islands it is still a flourishing trade, given an impetus by fashion in 1840, and employing in 1939 a thousand knitters. It lingers here and there elsewhere for the goods of speciality firms, but apart from the Shetland Islands and a few places such as Sanquhar in Dumfriesshire famous for its gloves, home knitting as an industry has almost vanished, swept away by the great machines housed in factories in the hosiery manufacturing centres of Scotland, the Midlands, and Southern England.

CHAPTER III
THE OLD HAND-KNITTERS OF THE DALES

OVER the brow of the hill they come hundreds of sheep like a great white river gathering momentum every moment, joined by more and more like so many foaming becks. Their cries swell and subside, then swell again in fresh crescendo. Never still, a little black dot tours round and round them; but it is too far away to see the movements of the dog, tongue lolling, belly to ground. A figure appears by an old thorn tree; and a whistle is borne away on the wind. In the dales of Yorkshire and Westmorland this, today, is as typical a scene as it has ever been since time immemorial.

We are interested in a small area situated amongst the high watersheds of the Pennines. Stretching from Richmond in the east to Kendal in the west—a distance of fifty miles—it includes Swaledale and Wensleydale, to the north Kirkby Stephen in Westmorland, and to the south Dentdale. The lofty fells of High Seat and Nine Standards Rigg guard the head of Swaledale; whilst Wild Boar Fell spreads its massive sides above Mallerstang and the Eden valley. Down the slopes of the hills splash waterfalls and rumbling becks, the beginnings of many rivers—rivers with lovely names: Swale, Eden, Rawthey, Dee, Clough, and Ure. These are lands of rich meadows in winding valleys, of high pastures and wooded gills—but lands where always the hills predominate. Near Sedbergh the Howgill Fells, hump-backed hills as sleek as sealskin, reflect the sunlight like shot silk. The only real giant of the Pennines that comes into this region is Whernside above Dentdale, though Shunnor Fell between Wensleydale and Swaledale, and Baugh Fell flanking Garsdale are proud rivals.

The district has no geological uniformity. The Yorkshire dale fells are of the Carboniferous Limestone series, and the Howgill Hills belong to the Silurian Rocks of the Lake District. Small seams of coal, of which Tan Hill is the most important, once provided limited fuel; and lead-bearing veins in Swaledale and Wensleydale brought an industry which lasted with fluctuating fortunes

Old Hand-Knitters of the Dales

from Roman times to the last century. The watershed, from which rivers flow both east and west, crosses the very centre of our territory. We are not even in one county, but straddle either side of these high lands, Yorkshire on the one hand, and Westmorland on the other.

Over the fells strayed the old Black-faced or Heath sheep, natives of the uplands since early times. Bewick describes them as 'a hardy, black-faced, wild-looking tribe, generally called *short Sheep*, which differ from our other breeds, not only in the darkness of their complexions and horns, but principally in the coarse shaggy wool which they produce. Their eyes have a fiery, sharp, and wild cast. They run with great agility and seem quite adapted to the heathy mountains they inhabit.'

Before an Act of Parliament in 1830 prevented inferior rams from being turned on to the moorlands, it was impossible to breed distinctive types of sheep; although in the eighteenth century the old Black-faced were beginning to be crossed with the Dishley breed of Leicesters, and were described in 1837 as one of the 'middle-wooled breeds.' From these original sheep have been evolved the Scotch and Rough Fell, and later by crossing with 'Mug Leicesters' the Swaledale, though this latter is too recent a type to enter into our survey. In the late eighteenth and nineteenth centuries the Scotch sheep driven down in great flocks to these fells were sold after a year's grazing to Lowland farmers.

In Cumberland were those ancient sheep of the mountains, the Herdwicks, which up to 1840 and later extended as far south as Orton and Ravenstonedale to Kirkby Stephen. They were white-faced, hornless sheep, though—perhaps due to interbreeding with the Heath Sheep—the rams, nowadays, usually have horns. The Herdwicks are described as having short wool, much finer than that of the Black-faced Heath Sheep. They are notoriously fond of their own 'heaf,' and 'sad home-wanderers' if sold and taken away.[1]

These two, the Heath Sheep, gradually being improved by crossing, and the Herdwicks, were the main breeds that supplied wool for the hosier. It can only have been wool of moderate length, and as such was suitable for knitting wool. If the hosier required worsted—a long staple wool—he had to import it from other districts. In those days, too, the sheep were salved with tar and butter instead of being dipped, and they were washed before clipping as washing increased the value of the wool.

---

1   See *Westmorland Agriculture*. F. W. Garnett.

The Old Hand-Knitters of the Dales

It is well to remember that Westmorland was on the fringe of the borders—the country of the foray and Pele towers—where villagers feared for their stock, and hid their valuables from the Scottish raiders. Here, until the end of Elizabeth's reign, the Warden of the Marches could call men to arms. Eventually the borderers degenerated into gangs, the moss-troopers, who plundered indiscriminately, and who after the union of England and Scotland were gradually suppressed. In the seventeenth century the lands held under the Crown by border tenure became settled—not without riots and lawsuits—into small farms owned by the estatesmen, later called statesmen.

On the east side of the watershed, in Yorkshire, much of the dales had been dominated by the abbeys of the Cistercians. Their extensive properties, granted to great landowners, underwent similar disturbances, involving lawsuits. Disputes between the landlords, the Crown, and the tenants gradually subsided; the estates were divided and parts of them sold; and a large proportion of the inhabitants became yeomen owning their land, in some localities under copyhold tenure. Some eventually accumulated more property than others, so that there was not the same equality as in Westmorland.

Sheep-farming was the abiding and fitting husbandry pursued over all the district. It was wool that gave prosperity to both statesmen and yeomen, wool that brought wealth to build many a stone farmhouse, whose carved doorheads and windows facing the fells, stand today as symbols of men's trust in the land and faith in the future. It was from the ranks of these people that the hosiers were drawn. As their dignified tombstones show they were men of substantial means, and in a few cases were the pioneers of the knit-hosiery manufacture, and carried on the trade in little mills housing machinery driven by water-power.

In Dentdale and the Westmorland dales most of the womenfolk and children of the statesmen contributed their share towards the families' incomes by carding, spinning, and knitting. As part of this self-sufficient life, home-spun cloth was woven and made into the 'gray-coats of Westmorland.' Lead-mining existed in Mallerstang, but on a very small scale.

In the north-west Yorkshire dales a similar self-contained life prevailed with the added and widespread occupation of lead-mining—an industry which drew together a larger population than could otherwise have lived on the land alone. Here, too, knitting formed part of the economy of dales' life.

Old Hand-Knitters of the Dales

The cloth trade, centred in the West Riding, never spread its tentacles to any extent beyond the Craven dales, so that in the country districts besides the lead-mines in Swaledale and Wensleydale, and some cloth manufacture spreading from the town of Kendal, there existed no other large industry except knitting. For over three centuries knitting was an automatic employment every day during all the working hours of many men, women, and children throughout the dales.

Time after time in old topographical works on the district knitting is mentioned briefly. For instance in 1780, Thomas Maude writes of Wensleydale: 'The commodities of the valley for home and foreign consumption, which last is not inconsiderable, are fat cattle, horses, wool, butter, cheese, mittens, knit stockings, calamine, lead.' Pringle in his *Agricultural Survey of Westmorland* (1794) says, 'Its exports are coarse woollen cloth, manufactured at Kendal, stockings, slates, tanned hides, gunpowder, hoops, charcoal, hams, wool, sheep and cattle.' It has been said that in Dentdale farms were bought on the proceeds of knitting; and about 1823 £40,000 was estimated as the yearly value of knitted goods in Swaledale and Wensleydale. When the industry ended it was, if only on a small scale comparable with the failure of the lead-mines, a cause of the depopulation of the countryside.

In the lonely outposts of hamlet and village traditions were carried on that had been long forgotten in the busier lowland country. Knitting was a traditional craft; and skill in it was passed on from one generation to another. It was no idle pursuit to be picked up at odd moments. 'Weaving,' an old dialect name for it, was indeed appropriate. The method is, in essentials, the same as that used at the present day in England, and is identical with that still practiced by the Shetland Islanders. The difference lies in the speed which is attained by a rhythmic motion and by the use of a knitting sheath or stick to support one needle. The knitter always wore a belt round her waist into which the sheath was tucked in a slant-wise position. We have seen many old well-worn leather belts, but not a 'cowband' which William Howitt described for keeping the sheath firm.[2] This, the name for the collar which fastens the cow to its stall, was in early days, of wood or iron, or twisted hay or straw. Howitt may have been meaning a band of the latter used as a belt.

The wooden knitting sheaths of the dales were usually the goose-wing shaped variety, and because of their interest are given a chapter to themselves at

---

2   See Chapter VII.

the end of this book. Other aids to knitting were the curved needles, called 'wires' or 'pricks,' which allowed a minimum of movement, and a variety of hooks to support the weight of the knitting. One of these was the top-crook described in the chapter on Swaledale. Another, called the top-string, was an S-shaped hook with a length of string fastened to one end, and the other end attached to the knitting. The string drawn behind round the waist and wound round the sheath held the garment taut. There were also a clue-holder to hold the ball of wool, and a broach, a wooden stick on which the wool is wound, tucked in at the side of the shoe or clog. We have not seen either of these, and latterly the 'clue of garn' (ball of wool) was pinned to the apron with a safety-pin, or suspended from the waist on a length of wool. We have been shown a goose's 'thropple,' the windpipe of a goose bent into a circle into which dried peas bad been inserted to form a kind of rattle. The wool was wound on to this, so that if the clue was lost in the dark it could be traced by the noise. Sometimes the ball was kept in a yarn bowl made of either wood or basket-work: this was put on the floor besides the knitter and prevented the ball from rolling away.

The children were never allowed to begin knitting without the appropriate implements and had their own small knitting sheaths. The sheath is worn at the right-hand side, and one needle inserted into a hole at the top, a hole that allows for a little play. The right hand is held on top of the needle with thumb and forefinger at either side, and the wool wrapped over the first finger which plies it over the needle. The left needle is held firmly in the left hand, and a finger pushes off the loops (stitches). 'Keep short needles,' mothers admonished their children, and meant, work as near the tips as possible. But the secret of the method is the rhythmic up and down movements of the arms performed so that the right needle 'strikes the loop' without the least hesitation. The body sways up and down in sympathy with this action which is something like the beating of a drum. It is impossible to do it in slow motion; and the loops fly off quicker than the eye can see. To cast on, the right-hand needle is used in the sheath to knit a stitch off a length of wool wrapped round the left thumb.

Sometimes the knitters repeated the old sheep-scoring numerals—yan, tan, tethera, etc. to count the loops. Thick yarn in its natural colour, called bump, was the wool used at least during the last hundred years. How the name originated is not clear, but it appears to have applied to the coarseness of the material. In these later days, the knitting itself was done on thick needles, and 'as open as bump knitting' was a commonly used simile. Expressions connected with knitting were in everyday use. One 'striving needles' meant competing to see who could finish a row first. An old man who died sixty or seventy years ago once told how he chided a friend who had 'got on and fancied himself.' He said 'Ah tell't him he needn't try to cu' lordan it ower me; it wasn't that lang sen 'at him an' me wor strivan' at knitten.'

It is a pity that most of the knitting songs, sung to pass the time and to encourage the knitter to greater speed, are forgotten. They appear to have been childishly simple and a Cumberland knitting song goes:

> Bulls at bay
> Kings at fay
> Over the hills and far away.

The old carding song once sung all over the North and the Lowlands is partially remembered at Gayle and Dent. There are five verses of which the first is:

> Oh! tarry woo; oh! tarry woo!
> Tarry woo is ill to spin;
> Oh! card it weel, oh! card it weel,
> Card it weel ere ye begin.
> When it's carded, rove and spun,
> Then your work is but hawf done;
> But when it's woven, dress'd and clean,
> It will be cleading[3] for a queen.

Wages for knitting in the early days were adequate to provide a livelihood: poor children were apprenticed to the craft. But in the decline of the industry the pay became very low. At that time the goods themselves had to be sold cheaply, or otherwise there would have been no market. For the men, the earnings were an additional income to farming for the support of their families; for the married women, they were extra money by which necessities for the children could be provided or precious tea could be bought; and for the girls or unmarried women, they were a source of an independent income. Undoubtedly the work stood between many people and dire poverty—though this was usually where large families of children had to be fed and clothed.

If over a long period knitted stockings were the mainstay of the industry, other garments such as caps, gloves, mittens, and jerseys were in demand. Of these the gloves which give a hint of traditional patterns are the most

---

[3] Clothing.

interesting. Adam Sedgwick speaks of the beautiful gloves knitted in Dentdale during the eighteenth century, and up to about twenty years ago patterned gloves in two colours were made there. Like the early Norwegian patterns they were originally obtained by using two natural-coloured wools from light and dark sheep. Of the few pairs which have been preserved we have seen eight, five from Dentdale, and the others from Cumberland, Swaledale, and Wensleydale. From these it appears that they were made over a wide area, and that they followed a basic design. The ground-work is knitted in alternate stitches of two colours, with in some cases spots on the palms and fingers, an elaborate pattern on the back of the hand, a band of pattern round the base, followed by a wrist-band with the name of the owner and lastly a fringe. In the later ones the fringe has become a striped welt. The patterns can best be shown by the illustrations.

The Cumberland pair[4] dated 1846 and knitted in natural and brown wools has the simplicity and charm of early design. The pair from Wensleydale which belongs to Miss M. Fawcett of Hardraw is the most elaborate. The name on the wrist-band is 'Mary Moor's' and the date is 1841. Mauve and scarlet wools have been used with green and white stitches in the centres of the pattern on the back and a green fringe. Three pairs, two from Dentdale dated 1911 and 1912, and one from Swaledale with no date but known to be about a hundred years old, are in black and red wools; whilst the remaining three from Dentdale are black and white, one wool and two silk and dated 1918, 1919 and 1927.

During the last century jerseys were knitted, called spotted frocks, which were flecked with stitches of a different colour. They remind us of the Norwegian *lusckofte* (lice cardigan) knitted in the Setesdalen. Of natural and brown wool these were speckled in the same way with single stitches over the main body of the garment. The idea for the spotted frocks may have been inspired by the cloth once made in Kendal called spotted cottons.

In our area Richmond, which has the earliest records for the industry, and Kendal, where it lasted the longest, are the chief centres. Most of the stocking trade was with London merchants or army contractors who bought up large quantities. As with all clothing fashion had its influence. When knee-breeches were replaced by long trousers; and in particular when in the early nineteenth century the British Army adopted the new style, the trade in long stockings received a mortal blow. Knitted goods from Richmond and Swaledale were

---

4   In the Wordsworth Museum. Grasmere.

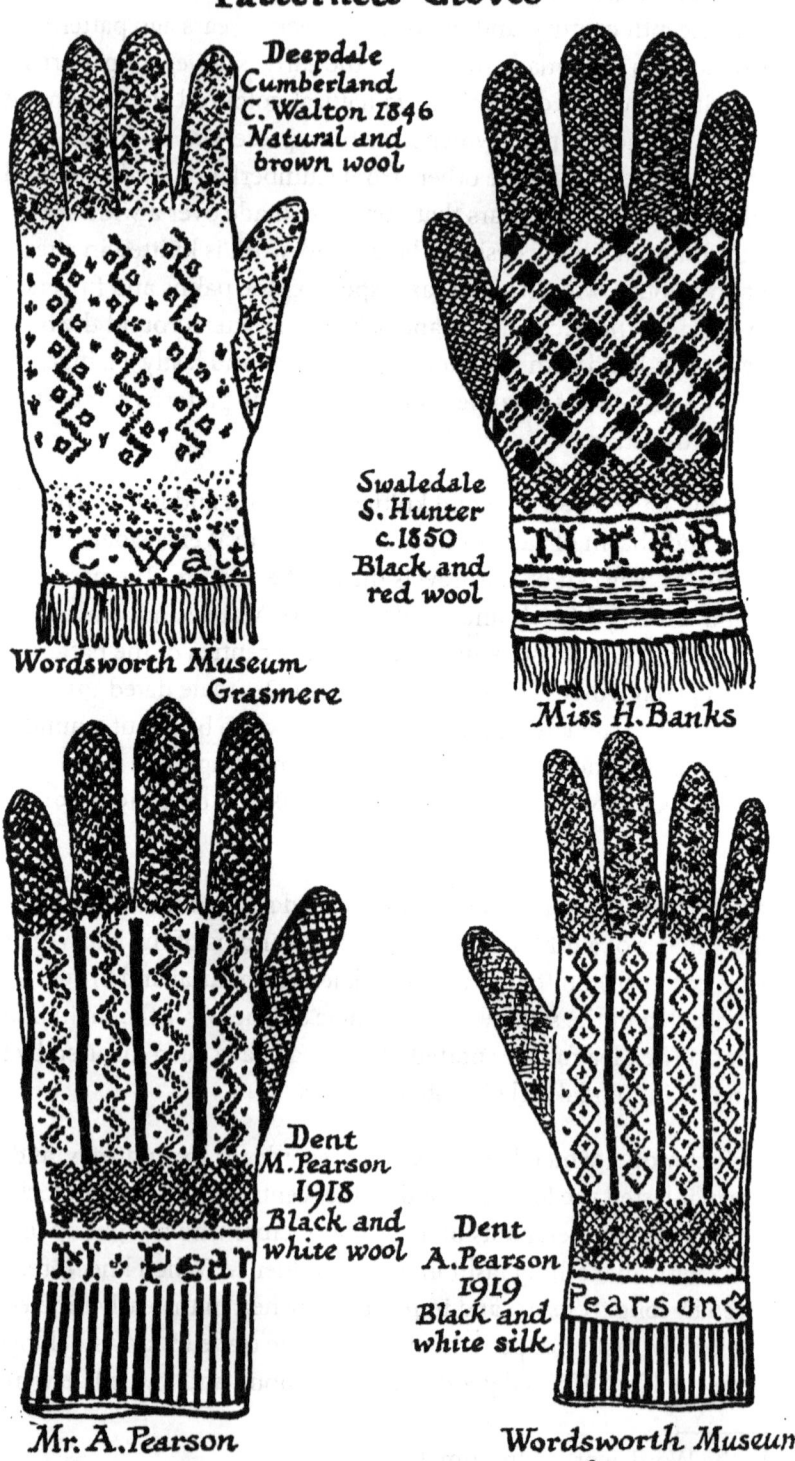

exported to the Netherlands, whilst the Kendal district developed a market in the West Indies and the American Colonies. There was a specified time of year for this latter trade; and we read of 'the autumn shipments.' A century and more ago sons of dalesmen frequently went to seek their fortunes in London, and occasionally acted as agents for relatives at home engaged in the hosiery trade. They seldom amassed great wealth, but their honest dales' upbringing stood them in good stead in the bustling, tempting life of the city.

So much for the background of our story. Through the eyes of many witnesses we shall visit the dales. We shall find grey stone villages, and in them meet families who have lived and worked there for generations. We shall be shown newspaper cuttings, diaries, wills, and account books, letters, family albums, and little treasured possessions. We shall see into the past when people worked long hours and lived in frugal homes, yet where the lamp of contentment burnt with a steadfast glow.

Typical Dales Knitting Sheath

Kilmarnock Cap or Bonnet. (Dick Institute, Kilmarnock).
Cap (2 inches long), 3rd century } by permission of the Victoria
Sock (Coptic) 4th–5th century } and Albert Museum.

Sealhouses, Arkengarthdale

CHAPTER IV
SWALEDALE

I. The Yeoman Hosier

IN our search for the story of the hand-knitters we must be prepared to move quickly through time, and our first stop will be at Richmond in the days of Queen Elizabeth. Richmond and Kendal were the towns round which the industry was grouped, and though Richmond yielded its importance in the trade to Kendal in later centuries it has the earliest records of hand-knitting. Both towns were proud and successful, and within a year of each other had Charters of Incorporation granted by the Queen.

Richmond was the palpitating heart of the large body of the farming community whose products were brought into the town for sale. The Guilds regulated the different trades, whilst 'Mr. Alderman' (the pre-cursor of the mayor) and twelve burgesses under Elizabeth's Charter ruled the town. Amongst the laws and ordinances we find: 'Mr. Alderman should have the use of the Wool-house, and the profits of weighing all goods there, saving that all inhabitants should weigh things freely.' This seems likely to have been connected with knitting because we also read: 'That no inhabitant was allowed to buy any knitting-wool in any other place within the town, than openly in the wool-house, there to be weighed, upon the "forfeiture thereof."' To prevent it from being engrossed and bought up for traffic it was ordered, 'That no inhabitant should buy any knitting wool for the purpose of selling by retail the same or any part thereof to any person, upon pain of forfeiture of it.'

We can imagine the families of the neighbourhood busily carding and spinning, and bringing the knitting wool into the town. At the latter end of Elizabeth's reign, poor children were put out by the magistrates as apprentices to the mystery of knitting, for no less a term than seven years under a penalty of forty shillings. They had to be properly supplied with meat, clothes, and lodging during the time of their servitude, for which their masters received from the Corporation about five pounds.[1]

Christopher Clarkson, the historian, compiled the above from documents that have since been destroyed by fire, but his account is confirmed by a survey of the industry drawn up by Thomas Caesar who had travelled over the whole district to obtain the information. The following is part of his record of the manufacture and sale of woollen goods in the county of York in 1595.

> RYCHMOND. In Rychmond there are above 1000 knyters wch doo make about 166 dozen every wecke they are in thes Townes nere adioyning vidz, Maske (Marsk), Sleton Gronton (Grinton) Marecke (Marrick) Midln (Middleham) Hipswell Barna Castell (Barnard Castle) Barnegam (Barningham) Hudswell Sandbecke Cirby hill (Kirkby Hill or Kirkby-on-the-Moor) Newsum (Newsham) Askirke (Askrigg) Buttersicke (Butterwick) Downham (Downholme) and Brenton (Brompton) as may (sic) knytters (sic) (vidz 1000) they wch are the marchaunts wch buye them confesse ther is made every fortnight 14 or 16 packes and every packe contayneth 40 dossen pare.
>
> Mr Person, James Metcalfe and Mr Trote (will) farme it of you, and wilbe wth yow this next terme, and if they will not deal wth yow, John Becke wilbe yor deputie, they wch kepe the greatest number

---

[1] *Clarkson History of Richmond* (1821). p. 410.

of knitters ar Mr Taylor, Thomas Arnot, Stephen Segwicke, Edward Pinckrawe, Mr Thompson, Mr Johnson, etc. accordinge to their owne confession of quantitie of dossens, it is worth per annum £32.10s. 2000 knytters after the rate of 2 pare every one a weecke amounteth to 333 dossen every weeke etc. 6/12(sic).[2]

The survey was concerned with the 'New Draperies,' which as we have previously stated chiefly meant different kinds of cloth as well as knitted garments for all of which duty was paid.

The 'Townes' mentioned in the survey are within a radius of twenty miles of Richmond, and all are small villages except Barnard Castle in Teesdale, and Middleham and Askrigg in Wensleydale. We picture almost the whole population knitting, as they sat outside the doors of their one-storied, ling-thatched houses, or as they walked to the centres to deliver the stockings.

The knitting trade went on without question throughout the seventeenth century. In 1724 when Defoe describes Richmond in his 'Tour through England and Wales,' he says:

> Here you begin to find a manufacture on foot again and, as before, all was cloathing, and all the people clothiers, here you see all the people, great and small, a knitting; and at Richmond you have a market for woollen or yarn stockings, which they make very coarse and ordinary, and they are sold accordingly; for the smallest siz'd stockings for children are here sold for eighteenpence per dozen, or three half pence a pair, sometimes less.

> This trade extends itself also into Westmoreland, or rather comes from Westmoreland, extending itself hither, for at Kendal, Kirkby Stephen, and such other places in this county as border upon Yorkshire; the chief manufacture of yarn stockings is carried on; it is indeed a very considerable manufacture in itself, and of late mightily encreased too, as all the manufactures in England indeed are.'

As we know that there was a considerable trade in Richmond in Elizabethan times there is no reason to suppose that Defoe is right in assigning the beginnings of the stocking trade to Westmorland. Doncaster, many miles to the south on the borders of Nottinghamshire, is given in Thomas Caesar's survey as having a trade in knitted stockings, and until the middle of the

---

[2] S. P. Dom. Eliz. cclii, 2.

eighteenth century the town was famous for its 'knit waistcoats and petticoats, gloves and stockings.'

Finally Christopher Clarkson ends the story in 1821. 'This town (Richmond) had formerly a large trade in the exportation of knit yarn stockings and seamen's woollen caps to Holland and the Netherlands, which through the fluctuations of trade and the vicissitudes of war, is now very much upon the decline and indeed almost entirely banished out of the country.'

For a glimpse of one of the employers of the knitters, we must turn back to 1680, and from Richmond travel up Swaledale, and at Reeth branch into Arkengarthdale. Here, high above the last village, Whaw, sixteen miles from Richmond, are four farms called Sealhouses. The largest of these has been the home of the Peacock family for three centuries, and is still owned by them, though at present let to a tenant farmer.

Whaw, a tiny village of stone houses that snuggles under a wooded hillside, is reached down a lane and over a bridge across the Arkle Beck. From it Sealhouses may be approached either by a cart-track behind the village or by a foot-path that strikes upwards through the meadows and over stiles in the walls. These walls, extraordinarily broad some as much as six feet in breadth, are built with great boulders of immense weight. Enormous black rocks are strewn about the fields on the higher slopes. Some are remains of buildings but most of them have been cleared off the land and left in gigantic heaps on the steep hillside.

The house is on the lower slopes of Kitlaw Hill and from it the fells stretch on all sides. The wild moorlands roll northwards to Tan Hill Inn and Stainmore, and across Kitlaw Hill a Roman road leads over the Stang to Barnard Castle. Away on the other side of the valley a moorland track shines like a bright green thread whilst the Arkle Beck curls down dale between lush meadows. There is bracken under foot, and all around on the hillsides are the 'deads' of the old lead-mines that once created employment for the people of Arkengarthdale.

A group of ash trees shelters the Peacock's home, a dignified stone building of the late Georgian period standing in a square railed-in garden. This solid large house has fine windows and lofty rooms and a staircase at either end of the building. Family tradition says that the present house was built after a fire which destroyed an earlier building on the same site, the original family home.

Swaledale

In 1680 we learn from a rental that four branches of the Peacocks lived in the group of farms called Sealhouses. One was Vincent Peacocke who had seven sons, John, William, George, James, Joseph, Vincent, and Benjamin. John, the eldest son living in this inaccessible place, was a yeoman who acted as middleman in the stocking trade. His family owned considerable property and was one of the wealthiest in the dale.

We find these details in rentals and in John's inventory and will made in 1680. At that time Dr. John Bathurst, physician to Oliver Cromwell during the Commonwealth, was lord of the manor of Arkengarthdale. He had jurisdiction over his tenants who held their lands by leasehold tenure, and presented their wills, etc., to the manor court which had right of probate.

When John Peacocke married, his father had made a will by which he bequeathed to him on his decease most of his property except ten pounds each to his other sons and land and houses to his wife. But John was to die before his father, and in his will he is anxiously concerned for the provision of his wife Sara and their child. The inventory made after his death is what interests us most and is worth quoting in full.

A true Inventory of all the Rights Credits Goods and Chattels moveable and unmoveable belonging to John Peacocke of Sealhouses in Arkengarthdale late deceased as they are appraised by us whose names are here-under written the 19th day of August Anno Domi 1680 as ffolloweth

		£	s	d
	Inp.rmis his Apparrell & purse	03	00	00
It.	one Tester bedstead & one trucklebedd	01	00	00
It.	two Ruggs two Happins (quilts), two pair of Blanketts two pair of Sheets two bolsters & two Mattrices	01	10	00
It.	two tablecloths, one dozen of table Napkins with one Carpett & other Small linnen	00	15	00
It.	one Cupboard & one pannell Chest	02	00	00
It.	three tables three Chairs & three Stooles with one Cradle & one press for Stockins with boards thereto belonging	01	10	00
It.	two formes ffower Cushions three shelves	00	03	04

		£	s	d
It.	two Kettles, two brasse potte & one Iron pot & ffower panns with all other ffire vessell of brasse & Iron belonging to the house.	02	00	00
It.	Nine pewter dishes, two flaggons, two Chamberpotte one Tankard & other Small pewter	01	06	08
It.	Skeels, Stands, Churns, Bowles, dishes & other wooden vessell with other Small Implements of houshold	01	01	04
It.	38 dozen of Stockins at 10d y dozen, some mens, some boyes, some for children.	19	00	00
It.	40 dozen more of Stockins at 8d y dozon	16	00	00
It.	two Stone & a halfe of wooll	00	18	00
It.	two Cowes	04	03	04
It.	one Mare & one Stagg (horse) of one year old	02	06	08
It.	one horse	02	10	00
It.	in Saddles Sacks & pokes (bags) with wheels horse tire (harness) & other Implemts of Husbandry.	00	10	00
It.	In Hay & ffogg	03	06	08
It.	Beef Butter & Cheese with one Gun & one pocket Pistoll	00	10	00
	total	63	11	00

The Appraisers names
James Kearton
Ralph Hutchinson
George Peacocke his mark W
Jo: Jameson.[3]

As can be seen John Peacocke and his wife lived in comparative ease by the standards of the time. Though he is described in his will as a yeoman, the stocking trade and not farming is his business. The stocking press was similar to a cloth press, and the boards—which we shall hear of many times—were flat wooden 'legs' on which the stockings were stretched. These were then put in the press in order to give them a finished appearance. The stockings

---

[3] M.S. in our possession.

valued at less than 1½ d a pair would be coarse and made from local fleeces. The description 'mens, boyes & children' is crossed out in the inventory. We may note also the sacks and pokes for collecting the stockings and the 'pocket Pistoll' essential to a man who travelled over lonely passes with money on his person. Barnard Castle was very probably his market town; amongst his debts is 4/- to a shoemaker there.

Following the inventory is a list of debts. £62 . 7 . 7 was owed him by fourteen people, and he owed twenty-four others £37 . 15 . 9 out of which £2. 14s. was paid in funeral expenses. £40 also was in the hands of his wife. It may be that these numerous accounts with different people can be explained by the system of barter. As we shall see the hosier in particular often supplied provisions in exchange for knitted goods. Some of these people, of whom ten are women, may have been his knitters. All are dale names such as Coates, Broderick, Kearton, Place, and Hird. They must have received infinitesimal sums for their work, and if any were the wives of lead-miners their earnings cannot have been essential to their livelihood as the miners received good wages in those days. So we leave John Peacocke, his stocking trade, and his wife Sara who has long ago, as he did, 'bequeathed her soul to her Maker.'

We now move back to the main valley of the Swale and pass up the dale through Reeth, Low Row, and Gunnerside, and a mile beyond stop at the hamlet of Satron. Members of the Clarkson family who live here have in their possession an old ledger which belonged to an ancestor, Joseph Clarkson. The entries beginning in 1729 mingle rents, personal items, servants' wages, repairs to property, and business accounts. These latter interest us most for Joseph Clarkson was a corn miller, a hosier, and a farmer on a small scale.

About the year 1733 he was in partnership with a Richard Hodgshon. Three mills are mentioned, Reeth, Crackpot, and Satron, of which the two latter have now vanished. He rented two of these, Satron and Crackpot, the former from 1741–61 and probably earlier, and Crackpot about 1737. He himself received a rent for Reeth Mill from other people.

These years were uneasy ones for the dalesmen. The Whartons who had owned almost the whole of the valley from Reeth westwards for two centuries lost their estates by the extravagance and eccentricity of Philip, the last Duke. In 1738 to pay his debts the manors were sold, and Muker which included the hamlet of Satron was bought by Thomas Smith of Easby and Gray's Inn. So we find Joseph paying rent to Thomas Smith:

'I am debt. for rent of Satron Mill due att Andrew day 1744
July 25th 1745 pd at Gunnerside £4 in full.
1745 Rent for Satron Mill due att Magdalen day
dec 5th 1745 pd att Muker £4 in full.'

The mill was west of Satron on the Oxnop Gill beck and is only remembered today by the name Mill Bridge. He paid rent to Richard Garth for 'Krackpot Mill' and in 1737 paid 6s. 8d. Crackpot Mill was on the Haverdale Beck which flows down to Low Row.

The most numerous items sold in the accounts are bushels of mash and pecks of wheat, stones and pounds of wool, wire, cards, and soap. Balanced against these are 'dozens of hose' received. The following is typical of the system of barter. (The dozens, of course, refer to stockings, and are added up and taken off the total).

Len John Widdow (debtor).

	£	s	d
Nov 18th due to me by account with herself	1	0	3
ditto 3lb wool 3s 3d. 2lb black 1s 6d		4	9
Ditto 2 bushels of mash 9s ¼ wheat 4d		9	4
Dec 18th 2lbs black wool 1s 6d 2lbs wl 2s 2d		3	8
Dec 23rd 2 pecks wheat		2	6
Jan 3rd ¾ black 2¼ d ¼ wl 3¼ d			5½
Jan 18th Recd 1 dozs mens 9s 6d & 2 doz boys 8s too dear			
ditto 2 pecks wheat		2	6
ditto 2lb black 18d 2lb lam wool 2s 2d		3	8
Feb 18th Recd 2 doz boys 7s			
	2	7	1½
(Taken off for the five dozen stockings)	1	4	6
owing	1	2	7½

Occasionally he remarks that the stockings are too dear, and in 1733 received a dozen from Will Metcalfe 'a very bad one.' Edward Milner of Thwaite supplied him with a dozen stockings, sometimes more, every month for four years. Others buy a variety of goods 'mutton 1s, brandy 6d, wine 1d,' all balanced against the stockings. He sells black, blew black, lambs' and once violet-coloured wool, of which black is the cheapest at 9d. a pound, and lambs' wool the dearest at about 1/–. The stockings are mens, boys, and girls—the mens are 9/6 to 17/- a dozen, the boys 8/- to 11/- and the girls 9/-. Though this is not stated in the ledger he would doubtless buy packs of wool, some perhaps imported and of better quality, which might explain the discrepancy between these prices and the ones quoted by Defoe. The wool was then sold in pounds and occasionally stones to his customers to be carded, spun, knitted, and washed, and bought back by him as finished garments. If the wool had not already been dyed, dyeing was one of the final processes. Cards at 1/6, wire at 1d. probably for needles, and soap 6d. for the washing are frequently found amongst the items sold.

In 1758 his daughters Margaret, Jane, and Nancy's Account reads: 'to have each £4 a year for all Manner of Cloaths, shoes excepted, and what they earn by knitting to buy their own knitting wool.' By 1759 his son Joseph is taking over the stocking trade, and in eight months £138 - 13 - 2 is paid out for wool and stockings. In 1760, £1 - 5 - 6 is paid to Addison for 30 dozen hose dyeing— Addison was a dyer at Askrigg in Wensleydale. By 1766 Joseph in his old age is turning over his affairs to his sons Joseph and James. Amongst Joseph's accounts are the following:

	£	s	d
Alex: Metcalfe hose	£4	12	0
Att Askrig 15 doz blew & black hose	7	3	0
leg boards.		5	0
hose in the house	29	17	0
in a further list, 2 pack sheets hose-pokes etc.	10	0	

Askrigg six miles south is often mentioned in the ledger. It was then an important centre of the hand-knitting with several hosiers and one or two dyers. Joseph probably sent his stockings to Stockton from where they were exported or sent by sea to wholesale merchants in London. The farming items of the list are worth giving for a comparison of prices.

	£	s	d
3 cows att £5 apiece	15	0	0
3 young calfes 15s apiece	2	5	0
2 sterks (heifers) 40s apiece	4	0	0
A why (cow) three years old	3	15	0
2 twinter whys £3 apiece	6	0	0
Bull Stirk	3	0	0
little bay mare	8	0	0
bay horse	5	15	0
Welsh Galloway	2	15	0
Mug tup	1	1	0

11 Scotch ewes 8s apiece	4	8	0
6 english ewes 10s apiece	3	0	0
	58	19	0

We could spend a long time with Joseph and his endearing little asides, his trusteeship of other people's affairs and his homely purchases. He was obviously prosperous, a generous master, and a fair dealer in his bargains. One account in 1735 is with the doughty dalesman, George Kearton of Oxnop Hall who lived to the age of a hundred and twenty-four. He sold him a ham at 4d. a pound, 13½ lb. of logwood (the only mention of a dye) as well as:

4 sto; ½ violet coloured wool att 13/–	£2	18	6
Recd in exchange by my wife's coat & some butter	3s.		

Many transactions are made by barter. 'Octo 12th 1744 sold and delivered to Robt. Hunter (of Keld) a red cow att £4 . 5 for which I am to have a stack of hay which stands at Beck Stones house end and 15s in exchange.' And again with the same person, 'Recd more a little table & he is to have a piece of oak in equall exchange.'

He sells his maidservant '2 yards ½ stuf of our own making about 3s' and lent his cousin 'att Kirby (Stephen) 2s 6d and bought for you a pair Little Shoes 6d, lent you a penny for the oastler.' One January he bought 'goose and apples 2s 11d,' in 1761 'pd to the expense of pewing the church (Muker) for two seats in the gallery 10s,' 'pd Frank for 2 days into Wensleydale & 2 days for making the clock-case 3s 4d,' 'pd for 15 quarrys of glass 2s 6d,' and 'for setting & seed reaping potatoes 18s 6d,' and 'a wig making 5s 0d.' After the transference of his affairs to his sons Joseph and James in 1766, the ledger loses interest, and becomes chiefly a rent book until it ends in 1892.

Hand cards from Arkengarthdale

2. The Last Phase

At the beginning of the nineteenth century Reeth in mid-Swaledale and at the foot of Arkengarthdale was a thriving town with market and fairs: a centre not only for the stocking trade, but also for the great lead-mining industry then vigorously developing year by year. The miners and their families all knitted both stockings for their own use and for sale. The thrifty ones often gathered fallen wool, and carded, spun, and knitted it in their own homes. An old poster advertising a Cattle Show held in conjunction with the 1841 November fair is preserved at Reeth. There are two or three unusual classes, one of which reads: 'For the best pair of knitted stockings of home-spun yarn. 1st Prize £1; 2nd Prize 10s; 3rd Prize 5/–.'

In 1870 a Captain John Harland of Reeth composed the poem *Reeth Bartle Fair* which begins with a conversation between two lead-miners who meet on their way to work. One says to the other:

> 'Swat te doon, mun, sex needles,' sed he,
> An tell us what seets te saw thar.'[4]

The expression 'Six needles' meant knitting the stitches of six needles, and was a commonly used and graphic way of describing a short interval of time.

One of the knitted garments worn by the miners and the farmers were long stockings without feet, called 'loughrams.' These were put on over other clothes in snowy or rainy weather, and because of the oily nature of the wool used, they turned the wet. They came well up the thighs—as one dalesman put it when speaking of the miners in particular, 'They needed summat to kneel on.' 'Loughrams' seem connected with the Scottish 'loags,' a name for a similar kind of leg-covering, and are also comparable with the old galligaskins, gaiters. In the West Riding they were called 'cockers,' another ancient name dating back to the time of cloth-hose.

Baines Directory of 1823 describes the enormous trade carried on by the hosiers. Under Reeth it says: 'The staple manufacture of the place is knitted stockings, of which article there is produced in the dales of Swale and Wensley, an amount of at least £40,000 a year, which is bought up principally by the neighbouring hosiers for exportation.' One stocking manufacturer, James Thompson, is given amongst the inhabitants of Reeth. According to

---

4   *English Dialect Society.* Series C. 1873.

the historian Clarkson, the trade had left Richmond at this date, though there were two firms of Spinning Wheel and Reel manufacturers in 1823.

The same directory under Low Row includes E. & A. Knowles, Manufacturers of Knit Yarn Hosiery. The Knowles family are connected with yet another phase of the knitting story in Swaledale. They came from the Keld district, and established a small fulling mill on Haverdale Beck near the site of the present remains of Haverdale Mill near Low Row between Reeth and Satron. This small mill had no connection with 'Krackpot' Mill which comes into Joseph Clarkson's ledger and which was higher up the same beck, and only used for corn. The Knowleses lived at Gorton Lodge and another branch of the family at Paradise, both large houses in Low Row. In the early years of the nineteenth century they carried on a trade in knit hosiery; girls were employed at Paradise where a room was built on for the purpose; and the knitted garments were taken to the fulling mill for shrinking and washing.

By about 1835 their trade had increased to such an extent that they were able to build Haverdale Mill, and to establish themselves as J. Knowles & Co., Worsted Spinners and Hosiery Manufacturers. This is the only mill of which there is now any trace, and the chimney and foundations were left when it was pulled down in the 1930's. At the time when it was put in, the water-wheel was said to be the second largest in England, and was made in the mill-yard of hand-planed wood. There are few remembrances of the mill's connection with the knitting; only that bump was spun, and that the garments were mostly seamen's jerseys, knitted large and afterwards shrunk to the required size. The firm also spun carpet yarn, and at first made carpets of excellent quality. But the force of water in the beck proved insufficient to drive the load of machinery. At length steam power was installed, and this necessitated the erection of a chimney as well as the employment of some forty dales' carts to bring coal from Tan Hill. Combined with the difficulties of transport to Richmond, these expenses reduced the quality of the goods, and finally brought the business to an end about 1870.

After this Haverdale became a corn mill for perhaps eighteen years. When it ceased to grind corn, it was used as a store for meal, and in later years concerts, to which people came from many miles around, were held on Good Fridays in one of its large rooms.

As the nineteenth century passed by the knitting and the lead-mining industries both began to fail. About the time of the 'Hungry Forties' many young men emigrated to the Colonies and towards the end of the century scores of families were compelled to leave to find work in Lancashire cotton mills and Durham coal fields. Those who stayed on earned something towards extra luxuries and their cost of living by knitting. The wool, no longer carded and spun locally, was brought over from Kendal and Askrigg to the upper dale. At Muker, Mrs. David Harker has told us of these days.

Her father, Ralph Fawcett, was the carrier to and from Hawes in Wensleydale, and on market days he collected a pack of yarn which had been delivered there from Kendal. As he approached the village with his horse and cart, people would hasten out and call, 'I'll take a bundle.' He delivered the yarn as far as Keld in one direction and Gunnerside in the other, and received ½d. commission on every pair of stockings. The garments knitted from bump were stockings, mittens, and jackets. All were made very large: the mittens came to above the elbow, and the stockings, called 'elephant stockings' by the children, because they could not think who they would fit, were a yard long and thirteen inches across the foot. Knitting the jackets was not liked as it was heavy work. In a large family the knitting was a necessity; but others would knit if they wanted something extra such as a tea-set. They received sevenpence for a pair of stockings, and three halfpence for the mittens.

Everyone knitted with a belt, knitting-sheath, bent needles, and a top-crook. They bought lengths of curved wire from the village shop, and sharpened the ends on a stone. Sometimes they might sharpen them on the jambs of the fireplace and leave permanent dents in the stonework. The top-crook was a small metal object which can best be understood by the accompanying drawing. The curved part was detachable at one end and hooked into the knitting whilst a piece of tape was tied in the round bit of wire below: this tape was carried to the left round the waist at the back and was firmly held behind the knitting-sheath. As the stocking grew the knitter pulled at the tape and brought the stocking round her waist. This tension helped the evenness of the knitting.

Top Crook (width 1¾ inches)

It is interesting to note that the hand-knitter supporting one side of the Framework Knitters' Company Coat-of-Arms appears to have her knitting draped round her waist in this way. Sometimes the base of the top-crook was made from an old copper penny, though the one depicted is of brass cut in a fancy shape. These implements were greatly treasured, especially the knitting-sheaths. The ball of wool was usually wound so that it unravelled from the middle when it was called a 'faus clue' (false ball). Mrs. Harker also has a bracelet with a hook attached to hold the ball though this does not appear to be very old. Everyone knitted with the rapid swaying movement called 'weaving' in Swaledale.

The Fawcetts had nine children. During the day the mother knitted a pile of mittens and left the thumbs for the children to knit at night when they came home from school. To pass the time they often sang hymns, or competed who could finish a row first, known as 'striving needles.' Or they played a game: as each came to the end of a row they called out the name of a person living at one end of the village, and so on all round the houses; and to vary this they named houses instead of people. How traditional it all is! The children of the 'terrible knitters e' Dent' amused themselves with the same game in the middle of the eighteenth century.

When dalespeople visited their relations in Lancashire they walked over the hills of Wensleydale and Wharfedale, and some times knitted all the way there and back. We were told too that Edward Stillman, Independent minister at Keld, famous for his walk to London in 1820 to collect money to rebuild the chapel, knitted as he walked along. Perhaps this explains why the whole journey only cost him 6d.!

An example of the skill of the knitters is one of the pairs of patterned gloves, described in chapter three, made almost a hundred years ago at one of the lonely farms at the head of the dale. They belong to Miss H. Banks of Askrigg, and were knitted by her mother when she was a girl. But for the most part fancy patterns were not for the old knitters to whom quantity was important. As a dalesman said, 'Knitting's like stone-breaking, you have to carry on to make owt.'

Low Mill, Askrigg

CHAPTER V
WENSLEYDALE

1. Askrigg

SOUTHWARDS from Upper Swaledale climb two moorland roads to Wensleydale, one of which is the Buttertubs Pass over to Hawes. The other, east of Muker, curves steeply up and up into the hills till at last the tiny white thread merges into the gray-green landscape. The tops are covered in heather; this is the home of grouse; in summer curlews cry incessantly, and in spring gulls nest by the tarn. Far, far below lies Wensleydale to where the narrow strip of road flows in a headlong descent. A broad panorama stretches from Widdale to Penhill, cool, spacious and fertile. The way continues to drop steeply, until suddenly round a bend appear the chimneys of Askrigg.

Although Hawes is now the market town for Upper Wensleydale, in the days of Queen Elizabeth, Askrigg had the market. It was included in Thomas Caesar's survey as a centre for the stocking trade—an industry which continued to flourish there until the nineteenth century. Richard Brathwaite, who was born at Burneside near Kendal, visited the town on his journeys in the north of England. In 1638 he published *Barnabae Itinerarium*, a long poem which described his wanderings. This was re-printed several times during the next century under the title of *Drunken Barnaby's Four Journeys*. There are two texts printed side by side, the one in dog Latin and the other in English, both written by the author. In the verse he wrote on Askrigg, the inhabitants are shown to be engaged in knitting, and evidently they were particularly busy with the employment for him to have noticed it as a special characteristic.

Veni Askrig, notum Forum,	Then to Askrig Market noted,
Valde tamen indecorum,	But no Handsomeness about it;
Nullum habet Magistratum,	Neither Magistrate nor Mayor,
Oppidanum ferre statum:	Ever were elected there:
Hic pauperrimi textores	Here poor People live by Knitting
Peragrestes tenent mores.	To their Trading, breeding fitting.

His English verses are often very free translations, and in our particular case the last two lines of the Latin can be rendered more truly as, 'here, according to custom, very poor people wander about knitting.'

Thirty years later after the Civil War, and at the time of the Restoration, fanatical adherents to the Commonwealth living on the borders of Yorkshire and Westmorland plotted against the Crown. The conspirators had a headquarters in Mallerstang, and one of them, John Atkinson of Askrigg, acted as an agent. The Yorkshire or Kaber Rigg Plot, as it was called, caused strong excitement locally, but failed, through lack of support, in 1664; and some of the plotters were hung at Appleby. In the proceedings against those implicated, John Atkinson was described as 'the Stockinger,' and an 'Anabaptist small tradesman.' He was well placed to pass on messages as he journeyed through the upper dales on his lawful business of pedlar and stocking buyer.

John Atkinson was not the only stockinger at Askrigg and one of his fellow tradesmen came to a tragic end on the very day that the Yorkshire Plot conspirators were hung. This was John Smith who had been buying stockings in the town, and had then spent the night at his father's house at Thwaite in Swaledale. The following day he set off carrying his heavy 'hose poke' over Tailbrig, one of the most desolate passes in the county, on his way to Kirkby Stephen. At the summit whilst he was resting, he was set upon and foully murdered. For another century and even longer there was danger from lawless characters for the unarmed traveller in lonely places.

These two men, John Atkinson and John Smith, very probably carried about with them other goods which they traded for stockings. A stockinger here seems to refer to the middleman and to be an early term for hosier, though in

Leicestershire and Nottinghamshire, the frame-work knitters themselves were called stockingers. The only other references which we have found locally, are in the Askrigg Parish Registers where the death of Guy Warwick 'stockiner' is recorded in 1721, and in a deed of 1670 'George Browne of Askrigge' is described as a 'stockiner.'

The eighteenth century is the era of the hosier in these dales. Fortunately for our search the parsons of that day recorded the occupation of their parishioners after entries in the parish registers. In the 1720's there were three hosiers at Askrigg, Warwick Tirrey, John Alderson, and James Birkbeck, and in the second half of the century there were as many as eight, George and James Burton, William Ewbank, Stephen Thompson, John Addison, Michael Smith, Edmund and Ralph Tiplady. There were not only hosiers, but wool-combers, weavers, and dyers. The dyers were often hosiers as well. For example in a small account book which belonged to a Wensleydale yeoman an entry reads '1758, paid to Geo Burton for a pare of stockins dyeing 3d.' The Addisons too were dyers, and as we know they dyed for Joseph Clarkson of Satron.

In early days red appears to have been a favourite colour for countrymen's stockings. Old recipes for a scarlet dye give 'skatchinele' (cochineal) as the main ingredient. But from the beginning of the eighteenth century blue was for long the fashion—blue for stockings, blue for cloth, and blue for aprons appears time after time in old account books.

The dalesman's dress is described by an old man in the early newspaper *The Wensleydale Advertiser* in 1847. He remembered that top-boots were worn when riding, and if these were not possessed knit boot-hose or stirrups, as they were called, were donned instead. These boot-hose were nearly always blue in colour, and were particularly suitable for snowy weather. He gives us a charming picture of old Willie Middlebrook of Countersett near Semerwater, dressed in breeches fastened with very bright silver buckles, lambs' wool yarn stockings and short gaiters; round his neck a white cambric stock and under his top-coat a white quilted waistcoat.

After the visitations of George Fox to Wensleydale in the seventeenth century a large Quaker community grew up. The Friends refused to pay tithes, and in consequence had their goods distrained and sold. The Minute Books of the Richmond Monthly Meeting record the assessments of 40–50 Quaker householders before two Justices of the Peace at Halfpenny House near Leyburn in the years 1761–1792. Their goods were seized, and sold at Askrigg, and amongst these were heifers, hams, cheese and stockings. In the year 1761 we read of the following:

John Robinson, for 2 years of wool	0	19	0
Reuben Harrison, cheese, ham, bacon and stockings	1	6	8
Alice Metcalfe, cheeses and hose	1	4	6
John Hunter, cheeses and hose and cash 'which he found by searching his pockets.'	2	16	6
Amos Robinson 2 Dozen of Stockings	1	5	6

On a June day in tile year 1792 a leisurely and observant traveller, accompanied by his servant, rode over from Barnard Castle into Askrigg, and stayed at the King's Arms Hotel. This was the Hon. John Byng, later Viscount Torrington, whose diary of his *Tour to the North* was published in 1934. He gives us a delightfully fresh account of what he saw, and says of Askrigg:

'People live to a great age here; owing to the fine air, and good water; and perhaps owing more to their distance from temptation: all are employ'd in knitting stockings, worsted, and yarn, an idle work, for the workers go where they like, talk, saunter, and sit down.—But now the cotton trade is coming in; and a cotton mill is built near the town, as many are in the neighbourhood. I bought a pr. of coarse stockings for my wet expeditions; or to put on when wetted; they cost me 8½d.'

At the inn he meets a Mr. Blakey 'who is in the cotton business, and comes from Manchester to establish it in this country.' Here and on other pages of the diary, we have a first-hand account of the building of cotton mills on beck and river in Wensleydale about this time. That near Askrigg is one now known as the Flax mill on Paddock Beck. But Mr. Blakey's projects did not succeed; and some of the mills instead, were absorbed into the knitting industry.

In the early nineteenth century there were two knit-hose manufacturers, at Askrigg, Thomas Pratt, and Jeffery Wood, and at Bainbridge, a mile away, George Coates and Wilfred Preston. Besides these, one or two of the older families of hosiers still continued in the trade, and of them the Burtons interest us most. George Burton who died in 1786 had two daughters, Martha and Agnes. Agnes married twice, first John Driver, and secondly Abraham Hastwell. Her first husband with two partners built the Flax Mill for the manufacture of cotton; but this was not a successful venture, and the mill was later converted to flax. John Driver died in 1787, and Agnes continued to have an erratic connection with the mill for about fifteen years. In the first years of the nineteenth century Mrs. Hastwell built the Low Mill at Askrigg, the third mill on Paddock Beck. Flowing from the high moors, clouded and brown with peat when in spate, the stream dashes down the spectacular Whitfield and Mill Gill waterfalls into the valley. The first mill on it is the old corn mill of the village, West Mill, now a saw-mill; the next is the Flax mill, of which part is now a farm-house, and the third Low Mill, situated by the road and close to a bridge, is today a joiner's shop.

We know little about Low Mill in its early stages, except that it was built by Mrs. Hastwell and according to village tradition was run by two women perhaps she and her sister Martha who was unmarried. Because of their family connection it would without doubt be a woollen mill, and was later called the Tumming Mill, from the dialect 'tumming' which means 'rough carding.' A gruesome story has been handed down from this time, of a man who, whilst crayfishing in Mill Gill, was bitten by an otter which clenched its teeth in his hand and would not let go. In great pain he reached the mill where they plunged the otter into the vat of boiling dye. It is said that the man never recovered.

Though the mill-wheel has gone the building has been altered very little since it was first erected. When it ceased to be a woollen mill in 1873 it was bought by Mr. T . Weatherald, the present owner's father, for a sawmill, and the main building was extended by the addition of a few feet, and a flight of outside steps built to give direct access to the upper floor. The original rooms of the two-storied main building where the machinery was housed measure 38 feet by 24 feet. In the ground-floor is at one end a large fireplace and at the other by the beck an aperture for the bearings of the water-wheel. At right-angles to this building is a smaller two-storied wing which would originally jut out a few feet towards the beck. Its lower storey was the dye-house and wash-house; and old flues lead up to chimneys on either side. The water was carried to the wheel by an over-head mill-race, and then ran through the mill under the dye-house floor. When Mrs. Hastwell built it, the work was well done: the king-post roof, the floors, some of the windows, and parts of a door are all original. The old belting that ran under the beams to drive the machinery has been moved to floor level and converted to connect the saws with a modern engine.

In the upper floor of the main building is a reminder of the wool manufacturing days. This is an old wooden crane which swivelled round through double doors to hoist up the wool packs from outside. The winding mechanism consists of two gear wheels, a wooden cylindrical drum for the rope, and three pulleys. The bell-like sound produced by winding it echoes hollowly across the years. All around are the trappings of a joiner's shop, yet the pungent smell of the fleeces which once impregnated the atmosphere seems to linger on in spite of the scented wood-shavings. Downstairs on a stormy day it is easy to imagine the shake and creek of the wheel, and to hear the clank of machinery, and the ghostly thud of a pack of wool being dropped on the old floor-boards overhead.

After Mrs. Hastwell, who died in 1835, a John Blyth of Hawes owned the mill for twenty-five years, and in 1863 Thomas Gill bought it. He is entered in *White's Directory* (1867) as a woollen manufacturer. The three sons of Thomas Gill were alive until John Gill died aged eighty-six in 1949, and William

Crane, Low Mill

Wensleydale

Gill, the eldest, died aged ninety-one in 1950. Mr. Leonard Gill lives in the neighbourhood. Because of their remarkably long memories we have been able to piece together the story of Low Mill which closed down as a woollen mill in 1873 when the boys were in their teens.

'Our forelders came from Swaledale, and we always feel drawn back,' said one of the brothers. Thomas Gill first came from the Low Row district to work at Smith's woollen mill at Hawes, and eventually started Low Mill with his brother John as a family concern. A Swaledale family, called Pedley, came to work in the mill, and they lived in the cottage still standing opposite to it. William was old enough to do half a day's work, and half a day at Askrigg school, and later at Yorebridge Grammar School. The two younger boys were given odd jobs. Mr. John Gill had the old wag bi't' wall clock that used to hang in the mill. They sometimes pushed the pendulum to make the time go faster, but did not realise that it merely made the swings of the pendulum longer. The older men noticed them, but only smiled.

Of the three mills on Paddock Beck, the middle one the flax mill has not been used within living memory. Low Mill the furthest downstream, though it did not need a large amount of power to work the primitive machinery, often would go for perhaps six weeks at a time without working due to shortage of water. At normal times the corn miller who had the first right to the water would let them know when he was going to grind. Many were the times that they started work at six in the morning in order to get the use of the water before the corn mill.

Plaids, rugs, and horse cloths were woven and yarn was spun for knitting. The horse cloths were made from the wool from black sheep, and the knitting wool was usually three or four ply. It is still the pride of the Gill family that all processes were done from the moment of receiving the fleeces of local sheep to the production of the finished article. Farmers also used to bring fleeces to be made into cloth for themselves, and then had it made up by tailors who travelled round from village to village. Shepherds wore the plaids which reached down to their ankles, and boasted that they could be out in the rain all day and not get wet. One such plaid is preserved at Low Row. Mottled brown and broadly checked with thin stripes of yellow and red there appears to be plenty of warm wear left in it yet. 'Things were made to last,' they told us.

When a pack of fleeces arrived at the mill Thomas Gill sorted it, the long staple for the cloth and short staple for the knitting yarn. Whilst doing this job he was covered from head to foot with flying wool. The fleeces varied enormously and depended on the type of grazing given to his sheep by the farmer. Sheep solely fed on heather produced very tough wool. The boys would hear their father say of the packs 'That'll be all right,' or 'That one'll be dirty.' He knew what quality to expect from each individual farmer.

There were five machines, three in the upper storey, and two in the lower. After the wool had been sprinkled with oil it was put into the 'devil' (the modern 'Willy') to disentangle it. This engine was so-called because it consisted of wooden rollers covered with iron spikes in shape like the traditional horns of the devil. Next it went into the carding· engine to teaze the wool into a smooth floss, then into the 'Billy' to draw out the loose cardings at the same time giving it a slight twist for the product to be wound into cops. Lastly it was spun on the 'Jenny.' After that the yarn was woven into cloth on a hand-loom and the rest was given out to the knitters. The finishing processes were the scouring of cloth and knitted garments in stale urine previously collected in buckets. Village slops were commonly used for the woollen manufacture before the use of ammonia. They were then thoroughly washed for they 'wift' as we were told, and afterwards stoved in sulphur fumes to bleach them. The knitted stockings stretched on leg-boards were put out to dry, often on the roof of an out-building near their house. Lastly, they were folded in two, and tied up in bundles of six for sale. Many hundreds of pairs were sent to Bainbridges at Newcastle.

They used to be very much troubled by rats in the waste, so eventually they obtained a cat. This cat was a great character and would occasionally go and sit on a stone in the beck to catch fish. One Sunday, Mr. Thomas Gill went to the Friend's Meeting House at Bainbridge, and was followed by the cat. It waited for him there, and when meeting was over returned with him to Askrigg. Sometimes the dyeing went awry, and Mr. Gill was seen in a pair of mauve stockings 'of a fearful hue.'

If any worsted was required it was bought from Kendal. They remember too having 'a lot of bright wool' from Dean's of Durham. Towards the end when the machines were getting out of date they obtained their supplies from Halifax.

The yarn was distributed to the knitters in half-a-dozen knots at a time. There were eight ounces in a knot at 1/6 a knot, and this was sufficient to make a pair of stockings reaching to the knee. Most of the knitters made an average of six pairs in a month. No check was kept on the wool given out. 'They knew nowt but straight dealing i' them days.' The stockings, knitted by people in their own homes, were large like the 'elephant stockings,' and were similar to our present-day sea-boot stockings. There were three colours, blue-gray, brown-drab, and dirty white.

Many women knitted in Askrigg, but by this time no men knitted for money. The largest business was done in Swaledale. Once a month they went over the hill-tops in a shandray (a trap with a covered compartment at the back) with THOMAS GILL, HOSIER printed on it, to deliver yarn and to collect the finished garments from people in all the little villages along the hill-sides around Gunnerside to Reeth. If one of the boys accompanied their Uncle John, he used to admonish them to give the wool only to the good knitters. 'I remember,' one of the brothers told us, 'that when we got to Low Row the women came running out like mice for it.' In the old tradition the Gills also kept a shop, and exchanged provisions for knitting. One old woman, however much wool they took her always wanted more; she never paid anything but 'knitted it all.' The lead-miners' wives at Hurst and Marrick knitted jerseys for the men from thick white wool, and this, delivered there the day after pay day, was always called 'groove wool,' (groove is an old name for a mine). The knitters earnings often went on extras for the children, but several liked 'a bit o' baccy.' Sometimes old women walked the eight or ten miles from Whitaside to Askrigg to a concert and knitted all the way there and back, 'to addle brass to git duds.' They were paid sixpence for a pair of stockings which after all the fetching and carrying and different processes sold at 2/4d. a pair.

To the boys these journeys into Swaledale were wonderful adventures; and in their old age they remembered vividly the old characters they met, and the hazards run in stormy weather. One evening their uncle stayed at Reeth and sent one of the boys back alone. Previously there had been a very bad storm; and the flooded river had swept away several bridges. However, the boy somehow managed to get his horse and the cart over a repaired bridge at Whitaside. Then a terrific thunderstorm started, 'far the worst I've ever known.' The boy was so frightened that he lay down in the cart, and let the horse find its own way home. One old woman when she asked about some material for aprons, 'Will it wear Jammie?' received the reply, 'If it won't, I'll fend it for nowt next time.'

Coal had to be fetched from West Pits seven miles away on the wild moorlands above Hardraw village. One time one of the boys went when he was quite small. As they returned snow began to fall, and became so thick that the child could not walk through it and had to ride. They struggled on, and at last had to leave the cart with its load at the bottom of the hill into Askrigg.

Old Hand-Knitters of the Dales

Eventually the mill closed owing to overwhelming competition with large firms producing machine-made goods. But the shop was kept on at Askrigg. In time Mr. John Gill built a new house and shop, and carried on in the old style a grocery and drapery business. He and his wife, who was ninety-one, retired in 1946, and up to then at the age of eighty-four Mr. Gill thought nothing of walking over to Swaledale for orders. 'I enjoyed it,' he said, 'but most people would find it hard work nowadays.'

A certain amount of knitting for sale continued to be done in the village. Mrs. T. Kirkbride who died aged eighty-two in 1949 remembers that when she was a child of ten or eleven she used to knit babies' socks in pretty coloured wools for which she was paid threepence a pair. She made about three shillings a month, and thought it a lot of money. She and her mother used 'to be knitting of an evening,' and if either of them dropped a loop, her mother would 'poke the fire and make a low,' so that they could see to pick it up. The wool came from Bradford to Hawes market brought by an Isaac Gill, a relative of the Gill family. Her knitting sheath was made for her by an old man who came from Swaledale to work at the Worton lead-mine. Since those days the tradition of knitting in Askrigg has lapsed although there are still many good knitters. A dalesman's daughters, whom we know, think nothing of frequently unravelling complicated Fair Isle patterned jumpers and knitting the wool up again in different styles. But 'things were made to wear then,' and we think of Mr. William Gill as he sat on the edge of the sofa saying, 'What a change! What a change!'

Wool Comb

2. Yore Mills, Aysgarth

Aysgarth is famous throughout Yorkshire for its waterfalls on the river Ure, and its lovely wooded walks. A steep road runs down to the upper falls and turns sharply to cross the river by an arched bridge. At this corner made by bridge and river is Yore Mills, a focal point of dale's life for over a century. A mile from both Aysgarth and Carperby villages, the mill and mill house, and two rows of cottages make a small hamlet which started to grow up in the eighteenth century. There was a pack-horse bridge here in 1539; but probably not a manorial corn mill as might be supposed. Early mills were usually built on becks rather than the rivers; and on this site the force of water presented difficulties only overcome by a long mill-race from above the falls. Aysgarth has an old corn mill, now used for electricity, about three quarters of a mile upstream from the bridge; and Carperby Mill, the 'lord's water mill' farmed at 33s. 4d. in 1546, was probably that on Ellerbeck, on the other side of the valley, where a mill stood within living memory.

In Tuke's *General View of the Agriculture of the North Riding* (1794), we read that in the years 1784–85 three cotton mills and a scribbling mill were built in Wensleydale. The scribbling mill may have been at Hawes, but we know for certain that Yore Mills was one of the cotton mills, and Gayle and Askrigg Flax Mill the other two. They all had varied fortunes, and for the purpose for which they were started were unsuccessful.

Whilst he was staying at Askrigg, Lord Torrington visited Aysgarth. He describes how he descends to the bridge and continues:

> What has completed the destruction of every rural thought, has been the erection of a cotton mill on one side, whereby prospect, and quiet, are destroy'd: I now speak as a tourist (as a policeman, a citizen, or a statesman, I enter not the field); the people, indeed, are employ'd; but they are all abandon'd to vice from the throng.
>
> If men can thus start into riches; or if riches from trade are too easily procured, woe to us men of middling income, and settled revenue; and woe it has been to all the Nappa Halls, and the Yeomanry of the land.
>
> At the times when people work not in the mill, they issue out to poaching, profligacy and plunder.—Sr. Rd. Arkwright may have introduced much wealth into his family, and into the country; but, as a tourist, I execrate his schemes, which, having crept into every

pastoral vale, have destroy'd the course, and beauty of Nature; why, here now is a great flaring mill, whose back stream has drawn off half the water of the falls above the bridge.

With the bell ringing, and the clamour of the mill, all the vale is disturb'd; treason and levelling systems are the discourse; and rebellion may be near at hand.'

In a talk later with Mr. Blakey mentioned in the previous chapter, he continues:

(He), spoke largely about the Manchester trade, now creeping, and which he comes to help forward, into this quarter of the country; and of the wonderful importation of children purchas'd in London, at so much the half score, (nine sound and one cripple) by those merchants, the most forward against the slave trade.'

This attempt to bring the industry to the people failed, and in the end it was the people who had to go to the industry. Members of many a dales' family, from Swaledale in particular, trickled across the border into Lancashire, and regular correspondence and exchange of hospitality continue to this day.

In its early years Yore Mills was run by the Birkbecks of Settle; but how soon it failed as a cotton mill is told by Whitaker in his *History of Richmondshire* (1822). When describing Aysgarth Falls, he adds a foot-note:

In my progress through this district I beheld many ruins with pleasure, but none, perhaps with equal satisfaction to that which I experienced in the sight of a ruined cotton mill, which had once intruded itself upon this beautiful and sequestered scene. I beheld it not only as the removal of a single nuisance, but as a fortunate presage that the tide was receding, and that an evil (the greatest which ever befell this country) is gradually declining. Richmondshire, however, though abounding in falls of water, has been fortunate on the whole, as in a tour of nearly three hundred miles I saw only two other defilements of the same sort.

However the mill was repaired perhaps by a Brian Sunter—though this is not clear—and was probably run as a combined corn and worsted mill. Some years later John Chippendale, corn-miller,[1] owned it and lived in the White House through the mill yard. At this time a school was held in an

---

1   *White's Directory* (1840).

Wensleydale

upper room of one of the smaller buildings. This 'Classical and Commercial Academy' was kept by John Drummond F.R.S., a mathematician of note. He was descended from the Earls of Perth who lost their estates after the battle of Culloden, when his grandfather is said to have fled to Bishopdale, and the family remained in these parts. John Drummond was still teaching in 1858 and issued a handbill which ends in the following quaint manner:

> The Friends of Mr. Drummond can testify to his genial worth as a Mathematical Teacher and Land Measurer: can verify with circumstantial proofs of the above insertion.—July, 1858.

Yore Mills, Aysgarth

In 1851 John Chippendale advertised the mill for sale, and a sale bill drawn up at the time reads that it is to be sold or let

> at the house of John Simpson, innkeeper, Palmerflatt, all that commodious Water Corn Mill 4 stories high, Length of the rooms 58 ft and wideness 28 ft inside measure, the two lower rooms is used as a corn mill with 4 stones, a water wheel 20 ft diameter 6 feet wide in excellent repair, with a kiln adjoining, and has at command the river Yore, the upper two stories have been used as a manufactury of worsted.

Old Hand-Knitters of the Dales

A newspaper cutting amplifies the description:

> Coach and cart-house, stabling for 8 horses, granaries, overlooker's dwelling, packing room, accountant's offices etc. Then only being used as a flour mill, but has been used for flax and cotton, and a great portion of the machinery remains on sale.

The mill was not sold, but part of it including half the house was let to John Sykes for £65 a year, and John Chippendale retained the use of the rest. This arrangement was short-lived. In the latter part of 1852 or early in 1853 a devastating fire, which was thought to have started in the kiln, gutted the main building. The owner faced ruin, and was glad to sell what was left to Messrs. C. Other and H. Robinson, local bankers. They immediately put forward plans for the rebuilding, and by the autumn of 1853 the roof was being finished. This is the present Yore Mills five stories high, and almost twice as large as the original mill. The lower stories were used again for corn-grinding, and the upper stories for the carding and spinning of yarn for knitting. So the mill returned to the traditional manufacture of the valley. In 1770, Arthur Young tells us that at Aysgarth, 'the poor women and children's employment is knitting and spinning by which the women earn about 6d. a day and girls 2d. or 3d.'

From Yore Mills the yarn was taken far afield into Swaledale and to Gayle ten miles higher up Wensleydale. A William Pearson who came from Bowes and who had worked at the Knowles' Mill at Haverdale, was the first manager. It is remembered that he and a John Hunter used to take the wool over to Swaledale by cart, and that some of the garments knitted were Balaclava helmets, dyed red and blue. The helmets were knitted all over the country for the soldiers in the Crimean War. Mr. Pearson's daughter, who was ten when the family came, married John Clark who succeeded her father as manager. This Mrs. Clark was a charming and capable woman who lived to be over ninety. She kept the accounts, and also acted as agent for relatives who ran a stocking mill on Coupland Beck near Appleby in Westmorland where Wensleydale farmers could get their wool made up into blankets.

The trade in knit hosiery was considerable, and one of the most interesting stories connected with it is that a large quantity of jerseys remained unsold, and were disposed of to clothe Garibaldi's 'red-shirts.' It has been handed down to descendants of the Other family that the jerseys were taken to Elm House at Redmire where Mr. Other lived, and were hung to dry in an outhouse, and that the smell of the red dye was intolerable.

Wensleydale

All the written records of this as well as the old people who might have remembered more are gone; and only a few relics of the knitting days at Yore Mills are left. One is a part of the carding machine, known as the 'devil,' a wooden roller about a yard long with iron spikes; also a broken leg-board on which the stockings were stretched, and lastly a shade-card for wools. This is a card measuring 15¼ x 7¾ ins. backed with glazed linen. It has numbers up to 62, and there are specimens of 52 yarns left on it. In one corner is written in ink 'Patons Alloa.' Though the shade numbers are the same as those used by Patons, the firm does not recognise it as theirs. The colours range from white, pale blue, blue-gray, fawn, brown, black, and red; and are described as 'Round Common Three Thread Knitting Yarn,' 'Coarse Yarn,' 'Fine Three Thread Lambs' Wool,' etc.—and the red wool is 'Pin Yarn.' It is quite unlikely that Yore Mills would produce all these colours, and if it did not come from Patons, it must have belonged to some other large knitting wool firm. Other people, we are told took their numbers, which became the standard for the shades made in those days.

The knit hosiery manufacture did not last for long, probably no later than 1870; but the corn-grinding continued. Mr. Robinson retired from the partnership; and the mill came eventually into the hands of Mr. James Winn. During this time dances were held on the third floor, and many are the happy

Spinning Wheel from Aysgarth
(Bolton Castle Museum)

occasions remembered there by older dalesfolk. In 1912 it was converted into an up-to-date flour rolling plant but was sold in 1927 to the Yorkshire Farmers Ltd. Ten years later under their ownership the mill was completely remodelled as a modern flour mill. The removal of the old water-wheel proved to be a formidable task, and it had to be blasted from its position with eight charges of dynamite. So Yore Mills go on grinding bakers', household, and a special kind of English flour.

The old mill bell, that has seen so much, hangs motionless now above the great buildings, its tongue no longer calls men to work, nor children to school. But below it the river roars on, water leaps down the falls, and to the bell perhaps the scene looks the same. Whatever changes are wrought by man, breezes blow down dale, and the pale-fingered sun brings warmth to cold metal.

3. Gayle and Hawes

Between Oughtershaw at the head of Wharfedale and Gayle in Wensleydale runs the steepest motor road in the dales. Picture a present-day traveller on an evening in late autumn crossing into Wensleydale. The wind blows cold on the summit as he climbs over Fleet Moss. At the start of the long descent twilight falls; and the first stars peep out from a dragonfly blue sky. When he reaches Gayle it is prinked out with little lights in the windows like so many glow-worms. The beck that streams through the village, icy and silver-flecked, mirrors in its rippling surface the last tinge of colour from the faded sunset. Geese, which by day march along its banks and bathe in its water, have gone to bed. There are no men leaning over the bridge or children playing; no housewives gossip to each other across the cobbled alleys. A cat slinks down Gaits; a man turns up Marridales; but in the Wynd all is quiet.

Gayle is left behind and Hawes is only a mile away. There the shops are closed, but in the lamp-lit streets people still laugh and chatter; and a lighted bus roars through the marketplace. Here once a week come the farmers from miles around to the Auction Mart. It is a typical little market-town where the housewives do their shopping, the youngsters go to the pictures; and where our traveller can find a bed for the night.

The houses of Hawes and Gayle in many cases have changed little from what they were eighty or a hundred years ago; but the lives and circumstances of the people who live in them have altered enormously. The inhabitants of Gayle were very poor. The men earned miserable wages employed by the

Wensleydale

larger farmers at walling and draining, whilst the rest of the family and often the men themselves, in any time they had to spare, knitted for a pittance in order to improve their tiny incomes. A sad story illustrates how knitting was a burdensome part of even the children's lives. A little boy sitting by the road-side talking to himself, was overheard wistfully repeating the following dialogue. 'Whar's Willie?' 'Nay, Willie he's gaen to whar its all Sundays and neea knitting.'

George Walker, in 1814, published his superb book *The Costume of Yorkshire*. One of the water-colour drawings is of 'Wensley Dale Knitters,' and a note in the 1885 edition tells us that Hawes is the background of the picture. It is a Hawes that we do not recognise. The knitters are grouped round a cross which no longer exists; and the church behind it has a sturdy tower, although Hawes Church prior to its rebuilding in 1850 had only a bell-cote. An elderly blind man sits on the cross, and about him are different generations of his family, whilst another man still knitting drives his sheep round a corner. None of these people appear to be using a sheath; their needles are straight; and they have not a ball of wool amongst them. The little girl has, dangling from her waist, a red heart-shaped object which may be a clue-holder for hooking up the ball of wool. We can only suppose that George Walker composed his picture from sketches (the church most resembles Wensley) and that he had not noted the method of knitting. For this deficiency he amply compensates by a first-hand account which accompanies the plate. He writes:

> Simplicity and industry characterise the manners and occupations of the various humble inhabitants of Wensley Dale. Their wants, it is true, are few; but to supply these, almost constant labour is required. In any business where the assistance of the hands is not necessary, they universally resort to knitting. Young and old, male and female, are all adepts in this art. Shepherds attending their flocks, men driving cattle, women going to market, are all thus industriously and doubly employed. A woman of the name of Slinger, who lived in Cotterdale, was accustomed regularly to walk to the market at Hawes, a distance of three miles, with the weekly knitting of herself and family packed in a bag upon her head, knitting all the way. She continued her knitting while she staid at Hawes, purchasing the little necessaries for her family, with the addition of worsted for the work of the ensuing week; all of which she placed upon her head, returning occupied with her needles as before. She was so expeditious and expert, that the produce of the day's labour was generally a complete pair of men's stockings.

'Wensley Dale Knitters'
from G. Walker's The Costume of Yorkshire, 1814

Kit and Betty Metcalfe
Gayle, Wensleydale

Bringing home the cops of yarn in
Dent Town. (c. 1880)

Although it is still possible to enter a cottage and find a daleswoman with her sheath, belt, and curved needles knitting a pair of socks for some member of her family, the famous old knitters of Gayle and Hawes have nearly all gone; yet two of the mills at which they worked and to which they took their knitted garments still stand on Gayle Beck.

The one at Gayle, now a saw mill, ceased to be run as a woollen mill a hundred years ago. It was built in 1784–5 as a cotton mill by the Rouths, an ancient Wensleydale landed family, and is one of those mentioned in Tuke's Survey. About 1834 the Rouths employed as manager E. A. Knowles, a member of the Low Row family who built Haverdale Mill. When it came into the market to be let or sold in May, 1841, it was described in *The Wensleydale Advertiser* as having been used for 'spinning of cotton, flax and wool, a valuable watermill, consisting of three stories in height, sixty feet long by thirty-six feet wide, containing the first movement of machinery, and well supplied by a powerful stream of water.' The rent demanded was £40 per annum. The tall houses on the Beck-stones were once combing shops for the mill, and are still known as the 'woolshops'; and near them is the eighteenth-century Clints House where the Rouths lived.

White's *Directory* of 1840 mentions Gayle 'worsted mill,' and describes Hawes as 'one of the seats of the Yorkshire knit-hosiery manufacture.' It continues: 'the knit-hosiery made here, consists chiefly of sailors' shirts, caps, jackets, drawers, etc., the knitting of which gives employment to many poor families here, and in the surrounding dales; but their wages are small, only about 3½d. being paid for knitting and scouring a pair of men's stockings.'

The other knit hosiery firms were situated at Hawes on Gayle Beck. The earliest woollen mill here was built by a family called Blyth who originally came from the place of that name in Northumberland, and who had been settled in the neighbourhood a century or more. This mill, perhaps the scribbling mill of Tuke's Survey, was at the south-east corner of the bridge in Hawes over Gayle Beck on the site of a present-day shop. They also built near by a group of houses surrounding a little square known as Dyer's Garth. To this day one of the houses is pointed out as the old dye house. Here the Blyths not only spun yarn for the knitters, but made cloth and wove linen sheets. A descendant of the family has both some of the sheets and a bagful of wool noils, dyed red and blue, that were made at the mill. In the early nineteenth century the Blyths travelled up to London by coach to visit the wholesale merchants, and brought back with them purchases such as books, shoes, and bonnets. After the family had had their choice of the bonnets, the remainder were sold. In the Hawes of that date a London bonnet would be an enviable possession. At one time, as we have seen, the Blyths ran the Askrigg woollen mill. They sent yarn by cart far afield into Swaledale; and a story is remembered of one of them overturning on the Buttertubs Pass.

It is possible that in the first quarter of the last century the Blyths erected Hawes Mill across the beck from the old premises. This is not clear; and the mill may have been built by the Smiths who were in business at Hawes by 1834. This large building now houses the Hawes electricity works, and a more recent addition to it is occupied by the Wensleydale Dairy Products Company. But we do know that the Blyths existed in the town before the Smiths, and how their business came to a sudden end about 1850 is accounted for by the following story. John Blyth had three boys who all died young and

Gayle Mill

in tragic circumstances. One went to a circus, and was attracted by the clowns jumping through hoops. When he returned home he tried to imitate them and fell and broke his back. The second son went to London as an apprentice,

Wensleydale

Hawes Mill

and was made to sleep under the shop counter. He contracted tuberculosis and came home. His younger brother caught the infection, and both of them died. The father, overcome by these three blows, lost interest in life; and his brother Charles without consulting him sold the business to the firm of James Smith & Son.

The Smiths as we have said were already established as hosiers in Hawes. They eventually took a partner named Whitaker who married into the family, and in their hands the business continued until 1904 when owing to competition from mills run by steam power it had to close.

Incongruously set amongst the lovely pastoral country, the gaunt old mill looks as though it has been moved stone by stone from the West Riding. Within sight of its windows is Spring Bank, built by the Smith family, a typical site for a Victorian manufacturer's home. The mill has three stories with rows of windows like staring eyes, and at one end, doors set one above the other. In the part that is now a dairy there was a large archway opening into the cleaning, sorting, and washing places. The boilers for heating water were between the two buildings. The wheel was inside the electricity engine room, its position marked by a tall window. Near to the wheel, stocks for milling beat up and down on to the garments. Here, too, was a large press which was clamped down on to the stockings and jerseys which had previously been fitted on to wooden shapes. The machinery including the knitting machines was on the upper floors. On the top storey is the old hoist worked by pulling ropes; but the attic once full of fleeces is now empty save for a few scraps of waste metal amongst which is a branding iron with 'S' on it. Wensleydale cheeses continue to be made at the dairy; the washing place is now filled with cheese vats; and the mill garth, where the knitted garments once hung on tenters to dry, is divided into sties for the pigs fed on whey from the cheese making.

Local firms were not the only ones who supplied yarn for knitting. The following item of news appeared in *The Wensleydale Advertiser* in February, 1844, 'on Monday night last, some villains stole from the wagon of Mr. Joseph Wignal of Keighley, a bundle of yarn weighing upwards of 50 lbs. The wagon was on its weekly journey to Hawes market, and was stopping all night at Aisgarth.' Joseph Wignal was a Keighley carrier, and was probably bringing the wool to one of the mills.

Later from the opposite side of the country yarn was brought on market days direct to the knitters from a firm at Kendal and from J. Dover & Son, Farfield Mills, Sedbergh. These mills used to send covered carts which both stood in Hawes market on the open space near the Crown Hotel. Here the knitters brought the garments each week and took back the yarn for the next week's work. 'There they were throwing them in,' we were told; and our informant added that her mother used to flatten the stockings when finished by damping them a little and either putting them through the mangle or sitting on them.

In 1890 James Smith & Son gave employment to about four hundred knitters at their own homes, and to fifteen or twenty in the mill. One of the best-remembered Gayle knitters is 'old Molly i' t' Wynd.' The story is recorded in *Wensleydale* by Ella Pontefract and Marie Hartley, that when the mill-owner told Molly that she would receive less for her next week's knitting. 'She just steud up to him, and said: "We've drained ye yer land, do ye want us to lime it an' all ?" '

'Old Molly' could knit in the dark so quickly that the click of her needles sounded across the street. In Gayle the rhythmic method of knitting was called 'wapping,' pronounced with a short 'a.' Once when the doctor was in the house, she brought out a long stocking and asked him, 'How would you like to knit yan o' them for a groat?' On another occasion a stranger wished to take her photograph, but she said, 'Nay, ah've promised to finish mi knitting

Wensleydale

for t' Kendal man.' But he persisted and took a photograph in a few minutes. 'What, ar ye deun?' she asked. 'Ah thowt you'd be scrowin' on for an hour.' 'Old Molly' lived until she was ninety-three and her spirit lives yet; for many are the affectionate tales told of her in Gayle today.

Though they did not knit for the mill, two knitters still remembered are Betty and Kit Metcalfe who used to sit on either side of their cottage door knitting cycling stockings with fancy tops. 'He was a jokey man, and people liked to talk to him,' we were told. Kit used a crude winder and a sheath made by himself, and he knitted the fancy tops whilst his wife did the rest.

Mr. T. Allen, to whom we are indebted for many recollections of Gayle, possesses a pair of cycling stockings knitted by these two old people, and a white jersey knitted by Molly when she was almost ninety. The stockings have yellow and green tops in a basket stitch giving an interlacing effect. The jersey made of finer wool than bump is obviously the work of a craftswoman. It is in stocking stitch with a narrow border of purl stitch bordering the V-shaped neck, and strips of purl at either side of the arm-holes. The whole garment including the seams and the edges gives an impression of professional finish. When Mr. Allen asked how much the knitting of it would be the old woman said, 'Well, t'others is yan and saxpence, but this 'es takken a bit mair te deu. Ye mun' gi' me yan and ninepence.' So he gave her half-a-crown.

Even fifty years ago large families had great difficulty in making a living. One typical Burtersett farmer used to work at Hawes Mill himself, whilst his wife did the farm-work, and looked after their thirteen children. Many were the times that she had to wash their clothes on Saturday night in order that they should be clean for Sunday. 'They had few changes i' them days,' we were told by one of these thirteen children who is now over seventy. When she herself was a young woman she went to work knitting machines at Hawes Mill. They made pants, jerseys, and linings.

Mrs. Martin of Gayle, and Mrs. Martha Dinsdale who is eighty-eight and lives at Appersett a mile from Hawes, are two of the last of the knitters. They remember men and women sitting outside their front doors 'wapping away.' 'We were fain to deu it,' said Mrs. Dinsdale, 'ther' wer' nowt else.' She used to knit sailors' jerseys with long sleeves, some high-necked and some open-necked, for which she was paid 6/– for six. There were also 'pop-jackets' or 'popped uns.' These had three rows of white knitting then one of blue making circular bands all round the body and arms. 'How many pops 'a ye deun?' was a familiar question. They used to carry the finished garments to Hawes Mill, and then 'lagged some more wool home.'

From cops brought from the mill the wool was wound into balls, round at one end and narrow at the other, with the wool unwinding from the middle. She used to pin the ball to her apron if she wished to walk about whilst knitting. When asked how long it took to knit a jersey, she answered, 'Ye 'ed to be a terble good knitter to deu yan i' a day.' 'When we got to the last,' she added, 'we began to think about the money.' She explained that thick needles were used for knitting bump and fine ones for worsted. She spoke of loops not stitches, garn for yarn, of wapping and bump-knitters, and recalled the days when 'Many a pun was made wi' knitting.' When we told her that we knit with straight needles and much slower than she, she laughed and said, 'They ought to 'a' larned ye better.'

CHAPTER VI
WESTMORLAND

1. Kendal

SET deep in the pastoral countryside of Westmorland is Kendal in the vale of the Kent. Traffic passes in and out of the town between Lancashire, Yorkshire, and Cumberland. From early morning when the workers come in to factory and office, the main streets are thronged with a crowd of shoppers, whilst near by the old yards down narrow alleyways dreamt contentedly in quiet backwaters.

From very early days the town was noted for the enterprise of its inhabitants in the manufacture of cloth. We find Kendal cloth-makers in the aulnager's accounts of the fourteenth century; and the famous 'Kendal green' clothed men in Tudor and Elizabethan times. Through the centuries the clothmakers waxed rich by the manufacture of these and cheaper cloths 'Kendal cottons' or coatings,—coarse woollens 'mostly white made in pieces 20 yards long.' These attained their greatest reputation in the seventeenth and eighteenth centuries, and were exported to America in large quantities. But fashion eventually introduced a demand for finer cloths, and these woollens were relegated to the use of horse rugs and house cloths. This trade was run in conjunction with the knitting industry in little mills in Westmorland, and in the neighbouring counties of Yorkshire and Cumberland.

The manufacture of knit stockings was introduced into Kendal not later than the seventeenth century. In a paragraph already quoted under Richmond Defoe, in 1724, found a flourishing trade 'at Kendal and Kirkby Stephen and such places in the county as border on Yorkshire,' and goes on to say, 'it is a very considerable manufacture in itself, and of late mightily increased too.'

Knitting was a useful double employment for people who could at the same time continue with other work. We read in *A Fortnight's Ramble to the Lakes* (1792) 'That both men and women were knitting stockings as they drove their peat carts into the town.' (Kendal).

Old Hand-Knitters of the Dales

This occupation of the inhabitants is pictured in the volume on Westmorland in *The Beauties of England and Wales* (1814). The author writes: 'A century has not elapsed since in the dales bordering upon Yorkshire the women often carried the dung hotts, a sort of wicker panniers, on their shoulders to the fields, while the men laid in groups on a sunny bank, employed in knitting, and no other way participating in the labour of their wives and daughters, than in filling their loads.'

Towards the latter part of the eighteenth century the stockings were knitted in a fine yarn spun from imported wool, and if they followed the fashion of that day they would have been ribbed stockings. Arthur Young, an accurate and careful observer, in his *Tour to the North* (1770) sets down a comprehensive account which reveals the importance and extent of the manufacture.

> (Kendal) is famous for several manufactories; the chief of which is that of knit stockings, employing near five thousand hands by computation. They reckon one hundred and twenty wool-combers, each employing five spinners, and each spinner four or five knitters; if four, the amount is two thousand four hundred; this is the full work, supposing them all to be industrious; but the number is probably much greater. They make five hundred and fifty dozen a week the year round, or twenty-eight thousand six hundred dozen annually: The price per pair is from 22d. to 6s. but in general from 22d. to 4s. some boys at 10d. If we suppose the average 3s. or 36s. a dozen, the amount is 51,480l.
>
> The wool they use is chiefly *Leicestershire, Warwickshire*, and *Durham*: They generally mix *Leicestershire* and *Durham* together. The price 8d., 9d. and 10d. per lb. They send all the manufactures to *London* by land carriage, which is said to be the longest, for broad wheel waggons, of any stage in *England*. The earnings of the manufacturers in this branch are as follows:
>
> | | s. | d. |
> | --- | --- | --- |
> | The combers, per week, | 10 | 6 |
> | The spinners, women, | 3 | 0 |
> | Ditto, children of ten or twelve years, | 2 | 0 |
> | The knitters, | 2 | 6 |
> | Ditto, children of ten or twelve years, | 2 | 0 |
>
> All the work-people may have constant employment if they please.
>
> During the late war business was exceedingly brisk, very dull after the peace, but now as good as ever known.'

The war was the Seven Years War, during which 'government agents were placed at Kirkby Lonsdale, Kendal, and Kirkby Stephen... 'for the express purpose for securing for the use of the English Army (then in service on the Continent) the worsted stockings knit by the hands of the Dalesmen.[1]

Arthur Young's day was the era of the building of turnpike roads; but prior to this Kendal manufacturers sent their wares by packhorse as far afield as London. As many as 354 horses in different gangs operated regularly to and fro into the surrounding country, and twenty of these went to Sedbergh, Dent, Orton, Kirkby Lonsdale, and other villages. Some of these packhorse trains continued well into the next century to travel over rough tracks to remote dales.

The way in which the trade was run is described by C. Nicholson in the *Annals of Kendal* (1861).

> The hosiers used regularly to attend the markets of all the towns, and at stated times all the villages and hamlets within twenty miles of the circumjacent country, to give out worsted which they carried with them for the purpose, and take in the stockings that had been knit during the interval between each visit. On the mountain side, in the valleys, and on every hand were to be seen
>
> 'The spinsters and the knitters in the sun.'
>
> It is supposed that the hosiery business was most flourishing about a hundred years ago, but we have been unable to obtain any authentic particulars so far back as that time. In 1801 the average quantity of stockings made for the Kendal market, weekly, was
>
> | | |
> |---|---|
> | In Ravenstonedale | 1,000 pairs |
> | Sedbergh and Dent | 840 |
> | Orton | 560 |
> | Total | 2,400 pairs. |

At the present time there are few knit stockings made here; other descriptions of knit woollens, however, are still, to some extent, manufactured for this market. These are single and double scarlet caps, Kilmarnock and plaid caps made principally for exportation to America and the West Indies.

---

[1] *Memorial of Cowgill Chapel.* A. Sedgwick.

The same writer says that 'a knitting school was set on foot' in the year 1800 in connection with the workhouse.

As in other parts stockings were knitted by the farmers and their families for their own use. These, made from local wool, were worn every day, but 'holiday stockings' were made of worsted.[2] The heels of the stockings were apt to be worn thin by the rough clogs, so the heels were smeared with melted tar then dipped in turf ashes which when mixed in with the wool became hard yet flexible enough to resist friction.[3]

In 1829 Kendal had twelve hosiery manufacturers,[4] some occupying premises in the main streets, others in the yards, but by 1849 they were reduced to four. The family of Edmundson was for long engaged in the trade, and they and H. Waddington & Co. established in 1864 carried it on the longest. The firm of Ireland & Edmundson, worsted spinners, sent yarn to Orton in 1868, whilst the Waddingtons took it to Dent.

Towards the end of the nineteenth century they spread their trade farther afield, and with the improvements to roads sent yarn to Hawes in Wensleydale, from where as has been shown it even reached Upper Swaledale. It is not clear which firm sent to Hawes. But here and in Dent the people knitted for the Kendal trade later than any other of the knitting villages such as Orton and Ravenstonedale in Westmorland. In an old warehouse off Highgate down one of Kendal's yards, the firm of H. Waddington & Co. is still carried on in a small way by a descendant. The knitting is now done by machines operated by two women, but in keeping with the long tradition of hand-knitted garments, sea-boot stockings and glass workers' mittens are the articles made.

2 *Manners and Customs of Westmorland*. J. Gough. 1812.
3 *History of Crosby Garret*, Westmorland. J. Walker Nicholson. 1914.
4 *Directory of Westmorland*. Parson and White. 1829.

2. Ravenstonedale and Orton

Twenty miles from Kendal, across the Howgill Hills, lie Ravenstonedale and Orton, small towns which vied with the famous knitting dale of Dent in supplying stockings for the Kendal trade. The two places once had markets and fairs, and led a self-contained life tucked away as they were amongst the fells. This country, like Dentdale and the Lake District was a land of statesmen who, towards the end of the eighteenth century through lack of capital could not survive the prevailing conditions, such as higher wages and taxes. Some emigrated, and some even became labourers on the land of their forefathers. They were replaced by the large landowner and the tenant farmer of the early nineteenth century.

It is these men whose passing Professor Adam Sedgwick mourns in his native dale of Dent, and whose decline Wordsworth notes at Grasmere and the surrounding valleys in his *Guide to the Lakes*. The years of their going with the consequent hardships and economic disturbances coincide with the beginning of the decline of the knitting trade which in these parts had been a vital addition to the statesman's livelihood.

Ravenstonedale, situated on the Scandale Beck, is a leafy oasis, warm and safe below the bare uplands of the neighbouring country. It was a meeting-place of old roads, not the roads of today, but tracks, called 'rakes', sometimes paved causeways, which ran in many directions up the steep hillsides, up Ash Fell to Kirkby Stephen, over Fell End and Bluecaster to Sedbergh, and west to Orton and on to Kendal.

The village had an ancient 'Peculiar Court' whose Grand Jury was composed of twenty-four influential men from the 'four angles' of the parish. In 1703 when Bishop Nicholson made his visitation there had been no beggars within the memory of man; but in 1729 the Peculiar Court made a new rule whereby elderly people applying for parish relief had to have an inventory made of

Old Hand-Knitters of the Dales

their goods; and in 1800 there were 156 paupers on the rolls. Amongst other goods one of these inventories contains the following items:

Household goods and other things belonging to Richard Robinson in the year 1729.[5]

	£	s.	d.
A spinning-wheel	0	1	0
Yarn windles (winders)	0	0	6
25 clues (balls) of yarn	0	4	3
A stone of wool	0	1	3

It must be confessed that these objects were probably connected with the spinning of yarn to be woven into cloth, but they are the same ancient names and implements that the knitters used.

Spinning Gallery, Newbiggin-on-Lune

5   *History and Traditions of Ravenstonedale.* Rev. W. Nicholls (1877).

Spinning Gallery, Adamthwaite Farm

When in 1801 the people of Ravenstonedale knitted 1,000 pairs of stockings a week for the Kendal trade, the population was 1,138, so that the amount was almost a pair a week for each person. In this year a writer in the *Monthly Magazine* pointed out that when harvest was over most of the labourers earned between 5/– and 6/– a week by knitting.

Some of the houses and farms in Ravenstonedale and the adjoining country still preserve their spinning galleries—often so called because both flax and wool were spun there. These were a feature of seventeenth and eighteenth-century farmhouses in Westmorland, many of which had originally no inside staircase, so that the steps to the galleries formed the only means of access to the upper storeys. Very many have vanished altogether, and the few remaining ones have been silent and empty for a hundred years or more. Their function finally ceased when machinery began to spin yarn in the mills, and when finer cloth than could be woven at home became the fashion. It is likely that of the woollen yarn spun much would be used for knitted garments. Approached by outside stone steps, these galleries are wooden balconies, sometimes under the eaves of the roof, and sometimes projecting from the main building with a pent-house roof and supported by rough wooden posts.

In the village itself there are two spinning galleries, one, now blocked up, on the Black Swan Inn, and another left open but with restored woodwork. Others are at Tower House, Brownber, at Newbiggin-on-Lune, and at Adamthwaite. It is remembered that some seventy years ago a spinning-wheel was still to be seen in the gallery at Newbiggin; and the owner of this has a ball of linen thread made from flax spun there. The flax was bleached in the yard below. Adamthwaite is a lonely sheep farm deep in a hollow of the Howgills. Next to its gallery is a wool-room still used as such. A member of a family who had lived there for fifty years said that she had known as many as three years' clips stored there. She herself had 'thrown up many a fleece.' Someone stood at the bottom of the gantry[6] steps, and another on the spinning gallery ready to catch each fleece and throw it through the wool-room door. She also told us that her grandmother could spin when she was a child, and that her great-great-grandmother always used to spin her own knitting wool.

Lord Brougham gave an election address from the gallery at the Black Swan in 1826, and was so struck by the amount of knitting done in the locality, and by the sight of the women and lads knitting whilst he was speaking that he suggested that the dale should be renamed 'Knitting Dale.' Knitting schools were established in the village, and one woman, Dolly Coupland, taught three generations to knit.[7]

From the beginning of the nineteenth century the trade in good quality hand-knitted stockings had slumped. After that bump instead of worsted was given out to the knitters, and it was mostly made up into coarse stockings, mittens, and seamens' jerseys and caps. The bump from Kendal was delivered to the Black Swan where the garments knitted the previous week were collected and returned to Kendal where they were washed and shrunk to the requisite size. A Mr. Allen of that town brought as much as £50 in wages for knitting each week into the dale. The people of the villages in the vicinity used to 'go forth,' as they called it, to knit whilst they gossiped and told stories during the evening at each other's houses. Some were so poor that to save fuel they went

---

6   attic.
7   *History and Traditions of Ravenstonedale*. Rev. W. Nicholls (1877).

to bed, and knitted under the blankets. The method was here called 'waving', (weaving) as in Swaledale, and a good knitter was described as a good waver. The people used to knit furiously, as if their lives depended on it, as indeed at one time they probably did. Though the knitting ended about eighty years ago and all the old knitters have gone, there are not many dalespeople's homes in which a knitting-stick or two may not be found put away in a drawer, and at Newbiggin, if you are lucky, you may still see a woman knitting as she walks up the street.

Although but a few miles from Shap Fell, Orton lies in flatter, more arable country than Ravenstonedale. Little becks, tributaries of the River Lune, crossed here and there by road and foot bridges, trickle quietly through the village; and paths lead through fields from one cluster of pink-and-whitewashed or stone-built houses to another. In Orton almost all remembrances of the knitting have gone, and the industry was dwindling away soon after the middle of the last century. In 1795 'women are mostly employed in knitting worsted stockings for the Kendal manufacturers, by which they earn about 4d. or 5d. a day';[8] and 'In 1868 there were six elderly knitters in Orton who knit 72 pairs of stockings each month for Edmondson of Kendal, when their united ages amounted to 478 years.'[9] The bump from Kendal used to be delivered, and the garments collected from May Bland's shop. She sold toffee and especially tasty kippers! Whilst in Orton we were shown several knitting sheaths. One was described as a good knitter; and its owner told us that her mother was able to spin. No industry survives, but it is still possible to buy hand-knit stockings in the village.

3. Kirkby Stephen

Ravenstonedale is behind us, five miles distant. Here at Kirkby Stephen our survey has reached half-circle. Away to the east are the Nine Standards above Tailbrig, and the summit of the pass from Swaledale where in 1664 the stockinger, John Smith, was murdered as he looked down over Westmorland. Northwards is the rich valley of the Eden, and behind it the ancient forest of Mallerstang whose fells, bare and calm today, are impregnated for ever with a turbulent history. There, Pendragon and Lammerside, southernmost outposts of the border castles, dream of fierce burnings, plunder and past splendours.

---

8   Eden's *State of the Poor*.
9   *Westmorland Agriculture*. F. W. Garnett.

Old Hand-Knitters of the Dales

But the flame of life that once coloured these crumbling stones has passed them by only to be rekindled by our imaginations.

Kirkby Stephen too has a castle, a mile away at Hartley, and a fine old church. Its market-place is long and broad, and twisting alleys lead off to back lanes, a typical plan of a town on the borders.

Though possessing a market for the neighbourhood since the 14th century, it never developed a cloth trade as did Kendal; and, indeed, hand-knitted stockings were for long its greatest and only manufacture. Defoe in 1724 and many 18th century historians of the county remark on the extent of the trade. Nicholson and Burn (1777) write: 'Kirkby Stephen is a considerable market town; noted for the sale of a great number of stockings knit there and in the neighbourhood.'

Kirkby Stephen carrier and his covered carts in 1817
Copy in ink of a wash drawing by Thomas Fawcett

The Stocking Market, Kirkby Stephen, 1817. Thomas Fawcett.
By permission of Miss M. Mason

Dent Town, 1810
From an old engraving.

Martha Dinsdale, Appersett, Wensleydale.
(Bertram Unné)

Westmorland

In 1754 a description of Kirkby Stephen appeared in the *Gentleman's Magazine* from which this account is taken.

> The market is on Monday, and as the stocking manufacture supplies the principal trade, this traffic is the first at the market; it generally begins about six, and is over about eight in the morning. Tho' the situation of Kirkby Stephen is under bleak and barren mountains, yet the communication with several of their own dales, and with Yorkshire, along the river heads, affords a pretty considerable market, an advantage which Brough near Stainmore has now lost for want of such connection.'

As has already been seen there was a link between the early centres of the industry through itinerant stockingers. No doubt these people brought to the town stockings knitted in Swaledale, whilst from near by places such as Crosby Garrett the knitters came in themselves with their goods. The stocking market was held on the north side of the market-place on the space in front of the present Barclay's Bank. Amongst the illustrations we include a picture of the stocking market as it appeared about 1817, sketched from memory by Mr. Thomas Fawcett, a former resident of Kirkby Stephen. He shows the housewives in poke bonnets, some with baskets of stockings balanced on their heads, and others displaying their goods for sale. A quaint verse accompanying the picture describes the scene.

> 'The honest group close to the stairs
> Has sold their stockings thus in pairs,
>   And all were knit by hand.
> They now return with their pittance,
> As each have got due remittance,
>   But small was their demand.
> This hard earn'd money thus was got
>   In winter nights thats long;
> Procured a cup of tea from t' pot,
>   And not so very strong.'

In later days the site for the stocking market was moved to Bewley's Yard behind its former site. The yard, so close to the busy street outside, is secluded and quiet, and with its worn stone archway and cobblestones recalls to mind the slower rhythm of an earlier epoch.

It is of interest to note in passing that in the late eighteenth century an attempt was made to establish the cotton trade in Kirkby Stephen. But the enterprise was of even shorter duration than similar ventures in Wensleydale; and the building erected as a mill became the Workhouse. The present saw-mill on the River Eden was once a carding mill. In 1829 Michael Faraday was a wool-carder and blanket manufacturer, though he does not appear to have included knitted goods in his trade. At the same time Anthony Dixon was a hatter, hosiery manufacturer, and tea dealer.[10] Very early in the nineteenth century long knitted stockings went out of fashion with the introduction of trousers, and the trade diminished rapidly, but continued on a small scale with jackets and caps. The yarn, thick and three ply, was known as 'Alloa Yarn.' It was so-called because it was spun at the place of that name in Scotland, where Patons, the great knitting wool firm, were first established.

An account of the knitting industry as it was drawing to a close is given by the Rev. W. Nicholls in *The History and Traditions of Mallerstang Forest*, 1883.

> Knitting was a universal occupation, both for men and women; indeed, it used to be said, when two young folks were 'wed,' that if they were good knitters they would do. The kind of knitting was the making of pop jackets and caps, such as those worn by sailors. They often spent an evening at each others houses, and this was called 'going a sitting.' At supper time bread and milk and cheese were brought out and put upon a 'coppy' stool.... Their work when done they took to James Law, of Outhgill, forty years ago. He kept a draper and grocer's shop, and the folks arranged to 'wear' their earnings with him. He took the knitted work to Kendal, or sent it by the carrier. In the spring, his wife, Mary, a woman of some character, made a special journey to Kendal, and brought back gown pieces, from which the women of the dale made a selection.... For these the women paid by knitting in the winter.'

Here and there in the neighbourhood of Kirkby Stephen just a few recollections linger. Some sixty years ago a spinning-wheel said to have been used by the last spinner in Westmorland was exhibited in a window in the town. It is remembered too that a famous knitter lived at Thringill Farm at the foot of Mallerstang. As was the custom she knitted by firelight and if she dropped a loop lit a rush-light, and blew it out as soon as the stitch was picked up. This farm-house has traces of a vanished spinning-gallery on one of its barns. But our way leads onwards, past Thringill and up Mallerstang to Yorkshire once more.

---

10   Parson and White's *Directory of Cumberland and Westmorland*.

Gibbs Hall

CHAPTER VII
THE TERRIBLE KNITTERS E' DENT

THE name Dent used to cover the whole length of Dentdale as it is now more usually called—one of the loveliest valleys in Yorkshire, well described as 'a wooded paradise.' Although in the West Riding, it is so close to Westmorland that even the architecture of the farmsteads with their white-washed porches and round chimneys is more akin to that county than to Yorkshire. Approaching the valley from the lonely moorlands of Widdale and Blea Moor, the narrow road plunging steeply towards Dent Town seems sheltered and warm after the bleak wind-blown uplands. In July the air is heavy with the scent of freshly-mown hay, and the banks are speckled with bright summer flowers. The River Dee twists and turns at the wayside, and below Cowgill, where the valley widens, the road splits into two on either side of the stream, only to join together again at Dent Town. Here is a picture from the past, a dream world of a hundred years ago. Narrow cobbled alleyways and houses built close together make blind corners and sharp angles on what is the main road to Sedbergh and Kendal.

Old Hand-Knitters of the Dales

Like the dales of Westmorland, Dentdale was once a country of statesmen who owned their estates with hill pastures for flocks and herds, and who were famous for their breed of horses. Many of these families became members of the Society of Friends, and led peaceful, dignified lives in their small ancestral homes. Equality blended with respect was the key-note of the relationship between them and their servants. But they fell upon evil days, and owing to economic changes these families gradually dwindled away. The dale population which had been higher than that of Sedbergh diminished after the eighteenth century, and especially after the decline of the knitting industry which had for so long employed most of the people. The Dent knitters were always the most famous of the hand-knitters of the dales, and today they are remembered with pride by the older generation.

Adam Sedgwick, for fifty-five years Woodwardian Professor of Geology at Trinity College, Cambridge, was born at the vicarage at Dent in 1785. He spent the first nineteen years of his life in the dale, and wrote of it, 'here is the land of my birth; this was the home of my boyhood, and is still the home of my heart.' We are deeply indebted to him for vivid descriptions of old-time life and the knitting industry in his little book *A Memorial to Cowgill Chapel* (1868). This was written as a protest against 'The Chapelry of Cowgill' having been mistakenly named 'The Chapelry of Kirkthwaite'; but in it are many recollections of the dale in the latter half of the eighteenth century, and of the customs, work, and way of life of its inhabitants. The book came into the hands of Queen Victoria, and at her wish an Act of Parliament was passed to change the name back to Cowgill. The following quotations are taken from his book. He tells how during the seventeenth and eighteenth centuries the dale was renowned for—

> What were then regarded as large imports of dressed wool and worsted and for its exports of stockings and gloves that were knit by the inhabitants of the valley. The weekly transport of the goods which kept the trade alive, was affected first by trains of packhorses, and afterwards by small carts fitted for mountain work.... Wool must have been a great staple produce of the valley, from its earliest history. The greater part of it was exported: but some of it was retained for domestic use; then worked into form by hand-cards of antique fashion (which in my childhood, I have seen in actual use); and then spun into a very coarse and clumsy thread; and so it supplied the material for a kind of rude manufacture, that went, I think, under the elegant name of *Bump*.

The Terrible Knitters e' Dent

But as art advanced, our Dalesmen gradually became familiar with the fine material prepared by the wool-comber: and, before the beginning of last century (17th), Dent became known for its manufacture and export of yarn-stockings of the finest quality. Some of the more active and long-sighted *statesmen* of the Dales, taking upon themselves the part of middle-men between the manufacturers and the consumers, used occasionally to mount their horses, and ride up to London to deal personally with the merchants of Cheapside, and to keep alive the current of rural industry.

At a further stage in the industry of our countrymen, worsted, that had been spun by machinery, came into common use; and the knit worsted-stockings were the great articles of export from the Northern Dales....

I regret the loss of the grotesque and rude, but picturesque old galleries, which once gave a character to the streets; and in some parts of them almost shut out the sight of the sky from those who travelled along the pavement. For rude as were the galleries, they once formed a highway of communication to a dense and industrious rural population which lived on flats or single floors. And the galleries that ran before the successive doors, were at all seasons places of free air; and in the summer season were places of mirth and glee, and active, happy industry. For there might be heard the buzz of the spinning-wheel, and the hum and the songs of those who were carrying on the labours of the day; and the merry jests and greetings sent down to those who were passing through the streets. Some of the galleries were gone before the days of my earliest memory, and all of them were hastening to decay. Not a trace of them is now left. The progress of machinery undermined the profitable industry of Dent, which, in its best days, had no mechanical help beyond the needle, the hand-card, or the cottage spinning-wheel.

He writes of 'all the knitting schools where the children first learnt the art many of them were to follow through life, and of 'the management and economy of the good housewives. A clever lass in Dent can do four things at one time, was said of old.

'She knaws how to sing and knit,
And she knaws how to carry the kit[1],
While she drives her kye to pasture.'

---

1 milking pail.

While speaking of the habits and manners of my countrywomen, I may remark that their industry had then a social character. Their machinery and the material of their fabrics they constantly bore about with them. Hence the knitters of Dent had the reputation of being lively gossips; and they worked together in little clusters—not in din and confinement like that of a modem manufactory—but each one following the leading of her fancy; whether among her friends, or rambling in the sweet scenery of the valley; and they were as notable for their thrifty skill as for their industry.

Their social habits led them to form little groups of family parties, who assembled together, in rotation, round one blazing fire, during the winter evenings. This was called *ganging a Sitting* to a neighbour's house: and the custom prevailed, though with diminished frequency, during the early years I spent in Dent. Let me try to give a picture of one of these scenes in which I have myself been, not an actor but a looker on. A *Statesman's* house in Dent had seldom more than two floors, and the upper floor did not extend to the wall where was the chief fire-place, but was wainscoted off from it. The consequence was, that a part of the ground-floor, near the fire-place, was open to the rafters; which formed a wide pyramidal space, terminating in the principal chimney of the house. It was in this space, chiefly under the open rafters, that the families assembled in the evening. Though something rude to look at, the space gave the advantage of a good ventilation. About the end of the 17th century grates and regular flues began to be erected; but during Dent's greatest prosperity, they formed the exception and not the rule.

Let me next shortly describe the furniture of this space where they held their evening 'Sittings': First there was a blazing fire in a recess of the wall; which in early times was composed of turf and great logs of wood. From one side of the fire-place ran a bench, with a strong and sometimes ornamentally carved back, called a *lang settle*. On the other side of the fire-place was the Patriarch's wooden and well carved arm-chair; and near the chair was the *sconce* adorned with crockery. Not far off was commonly seen a well-carved cupboard, or cabinet, marked with some date that fell within a period of fifty years after the restoration of Charles the Second; and fixed to the beams of the upper floor was a row of cupboards, called the *Cat-malison* (the cat's curse); because from its position it was secure from poor grimalkin's paw. One or two small tables, together with chairs or benches, gave seats to all the party there assembled. Rude though the room appeared, there was in it no sign of want. It had many signs of rural comfort: for under the rafters were suspended bunches of herbs for cookery, hams sometimes for export, flitches of bacon, legs of beef, and other articles salted for domestic use.

They took their seats; and then began the work of the evening; and with a speed that cheated the eye they went on with their respective tasks. Beautiful gloves were thrown off complete; and worsted stockings made good progress. There was no dreary deafening noise of machinery; but there was the merry heart-cheering sound of the human tongue. No one could foretell the current of the evening's talk. They had their ghost tales; and their love tales; and their battles of jests and riddles; and their ancient songs of enormous length, yet heard by ears that were never weary. Each in turn was to play its part, according to the humour of the *Sitting*. Or by way of change, some lassie who was bright and *renable* was asked to read for the amusement of the party. She would sit down; and, apparently without interrupting her work by more than a single stitch, would begin to read—for example, a chapter of *Robinson Crusoe*. In a moment the confusion of sounds ceased: and no sound was heard but the reader's voice, and the click of the knitting needles, while she herself went on knitting: and she would turn over the leaves before her (as a lady does those of her music-book from the stool of her piano), hardly losing a second at each successive leaf, till the chapter was done. Or at another and graver party, some one, perhaps, would read a chapter from the *Pilgrim's Progress*. It also charmed all tongues to silence: but, as certainly, led to a grave discussion so soon as the reading ceased.

I am not drawing from my imagination, but from the memory of what I have seen and heard in my younger, school-boy days; and I only knew Dent while in its decline. Such were the happy family 'Sittings,' in which labour and sorrow were divorced, and labour and joy were for a while united.'

The fame of the Dent knitters reached even the Lake Poets. In a chapter of his miscellany *The Doctor* (1834–37), Robert Southey gave them a title which has become a by-word whenever knitting is mentioned in the dales. 'They er terrible knitters e' Dent,' he wrote. His title has been popularised into 'The terrible knitters of Dent,' though the correct rendering from the dialect is,

Old Hand-Knitters of the Dales

'The great knitters in Dent.'[2] Southey's story was taken down from the lips of an elderly woman, Betty Yewdale of Rydal, by Sarah Hutchinson, Mrs. Wordsworth's sister and a Mrs. Warter. Wordsworth also writes of her and her husband, the quarryman, in *The Excursion*, Book 5; and her daughter was employed by the Wordsworths as a maid.

The tale is told in dialect and describes an episode in the old woman's childhood about 1760. At that time a woman from Dent came to Langdale where the Yewdales lived. The father and mother, wishing to have their children taught to knit, sent their two little girls, Betty aged seven or eight and Sally, two years younger, back to Dentdale. With the woman and a man they travelled on horse-back to a house about four miles above Dent Town. Although treated kindly they were bitterly homesick. They disliked the coarse food—chiefly havercakes—'round Meal—an they stoult[3] it int' frying-pan, e' keeaks as thick as my finger.'

> Then we were stawed[4] we sae mickle knitting—We went to a Skeul about a mile off—ther wa sa Maister an Mistress—they larnt us our lessons, yan a piece—an' then we o' knit as hard as we cud drive, striving which cud knit t' hardest yan against anudder—We hed our Darracks[5] set afore we come fra' Heam int' mwornin; an' if we deedn't git them duun we warrant to gang to our dinners—They hed o' macks o' contrivances to larn us to knit swift—T' maister wad wind 3 or 4 clues togedder, for 3 or 4 Bairns to knit off—*that* at knit slawest raffled tudders yarn, an' than she gat weel thumpt (but ther was baith Lasses an' Lads 'at learnt at knit)—Than we ust at sing a mack of a sang, whilk we wer at git at t'end on at every needle, ca'ing ower t 'Neams of o' t' fwoak in t' Deeal—but Sally an me wad never ca' Dent fwoak—sea we ca'ed Langdon Fwoak—T' Sang was—
>
> Sally an' I, Sally an' I,
> For a good pudding pye,
> Taa hoaf wheat, an' tudder hoaf rye,
> Sally an' I, for a good pudding pye.
>
> We sang this (altering t' neams) at every needle: and when we com at t' end cried 'off' an' began again, an' sea *we strave* on o' t' day through

---

2   'terrible' can also be used as an adverb when it means 'very'.
3   threw roughly.
4   saturated.
5   day's work.

The Terrible Knitters e' Dent

Neet an' Day ther was nought but *this* knitting! T' Nebbors ust at gang about fra' house to house, we' ther wark,—than yan fire dud, ye knaw, an' they cud hev a better—they had girt lang black peeats.... When ony o' them gat into a hubble we ther wark, they shouted out 'turn a Peeat'—an' *them* 'at sat naarest t' fire turnt yan, an' meaad a low—for they nivver hed onny cannal[6].—We knit quorse wosset stockings—some gloves—an' some neet caps, an' wastecwoat breests an' petticwoats. I yance knat a stocking, for mysell, e' six hours.

At last, one cold winter evening with snow on the ground, the children ran away. They had only sixpence between them, and were scantily clad in hats, blue bedgowns (short print jackets), and brats (aprons). At 'Scotch Jins' public-house, about three miles from Sedbergh, they were able to spend the night. When they reached Kendal the following evening, a poor woman took pity on them, but put them to sleep in a bedroom with an old woman who had fits. Betty remembered that her face turned black, and that she and her sister were terrified—Next morning they trudged on again towards Langdale, and in the end reached home about two in the morning. Southey might well have called his tale the terrible adventures of Betty and Sally Yewdale.

In the early part of the last century William and Mary Howitt, on their travels, came to Dentdale where they had Quaker relatives. Mary Howitt brings the knitters into her novel *Hope on, Hope ever*, which is set at Gibb's Hall near Dent Town, and William Howitt in *The Rural Life of England* (1844) takes Dentdale as a specimen of the Northern Dales when he describes what he calls 'These retired regions.' His portrayal of the knitters amplifies and complements the picture given us by Adam Sedgwick and Robert Southey.

> But perhaps the most characteristic custom of the Dales is what is called their Sitting, or going-a-sitting. Knitting is a great practice in the dales. Men, women, and children, all knit. Formerly you might have met the wagoners knitting as they went along with their teams; but this is now rare; for the greater influx of visitors, and their wonder expressed at this and other practices, has made them rather ashamed of some of them, and shy of strangers observing them. But the men still knit a great deal in the houses; and the women knit incessantly. They have knitting schools, where the children are taught; and where they sing in chorus knitting songs, some of which appear as childish as the nursery stories of the last generation. Yet all of them bear some

---

6   candle.

reference to their employment and mode of life; and the chorus, which maintains regularity of action and keeps up the attention, is of more importance than the words. Here is a specimen.

> Bell-wether o' Barking, cries baa, baa,
> How many sheep have we lost to-day?
> Nineteen have we lost, one have we fun,
> Run Rockie, run Rockie, run, run, run.[7]

This is sung while they knit one round of the stocking; when the second round commences they begin again—

> Bell-wether o' Barking, cries baa, baa,
> How many sheep have we lost to-day?
> Eighteen have we lost, two have we fun,
> Run Rockie, run Rockie, run, run, run;

and so on till they have knit twenty rounds, decreasing the numbers on the one hand, and increasing them on the other. These songs are sung not only by the children in the schools, but also by the people at their sittings, which are social assemblies of the neighbourhood, not for eating and drinking, but merely for society. As soon as it becomes dark, and the usual business of the day is over, and the young children are put to bed, they rake or put out the fire; take their cloaks and lanterns, and set out with their knitting to the house of the neighbour where the sitting falls in rotation, for it is a regularly circulating assembly from house to house through the particular neighbourhood. The whole troop of neighbours being collected, they sit and knit, sing knitting-songs, and tell knitting-stories. Here all the old stories and traditions of the dale come up, and they often get so excited that they say, 'Neighbours, we'll not part to-night,' that is, till after twelve o'clock. All this time their knitting goes on with unremitting speed. They sit rocking to and fro like so many weird wizards. They burn no candle, but knit by the light of the peat fire. And this rocking motion is connected with a mode of knitting peculiar to the place, called swaving, which is difficult to describe. Ordinary knitting is performed by a variety of little motions, but this is a single uniform tossing motion of both the hands at once, and the body often accompanying it with a sort of sympathetic action. The knitting produced is just the same as by the ordinary method. They knit with crooked pins called

---

[7]   A Bell-wether is a sheep with a bell tied round its neck, the leader of a flock; Barking is a hill overlooking Dent, and Rockie a sheep dog.

pricks; and use a knitting-sheath consisting commonly of a hollow piece of wood,[8] as large as the sheath of a dagger, curved to the side, and fixed in a belt called the cowband. The women of the north, in fact, often sport very curious knitting-sheaths. We have seen a wisp of straw tied up pretty tightly, into which they stick their needles; and sometimes a bunch of quills of at least half-a-hundred in number. These sheaths and cowbands are often presents from their lovers to the young women. Upon the band there is a hook, upon which the long end of the knitting is suspended that it may not dangle. In this manner they knit for the Kendal market, stockings, jackets, nightcaps, and a kind of caps worn by the negroes, called bump-caps. These are made of very coarse worsted, and knit a yard in length, one half of which is turned into the others, before it has the appearance of a cap.

The smallness of their earnings may be inferred from the price for the knitting of one of these caps being threepence. But all knit, and knitting is not so much their sole labour as an auxiliary gain. The woman knits when her household work is done; the man when his out-of-door work is done; as they walk about their garden, or go from one village to another, the process is going on. We saw a stout rosy girl driving some cows to the field. She had all the character of a farmer's servant. Without anything on her head, in her short bed-gown and wooden clogs, she went on after them with a great stick in her hand. A lot of calves which were in the field, as she opened the gate, seemed determined to rush out, but the damsel laid lustily about them with her cudgel, and made them decamp. As we observed her proceedings from a house opposite, and, amused at the contest between her and the calves, said, 'Well done! dairymaid!' 'O,' said the woman of the house, 'that is no dairymaid: she is the farmer's only daughter, and will have quite a fortune. She is the best knitter in the dale, and makes four bump-caps a day'; that is, the young lady of fortune earned a shilling a day.

'In Deep-dale, (near Dent) the farmers principally employ themselves at home in sorting and carding wool for knitting. They call it *welding*; and the fine locks, selected for the legs of the stockings, they call *leggin*, whilst the coarser part goes by the name of *footing*. Two old people, Laurence and Peggy Hodson o'Dockensyke, were both upwards of seventy, when Peggy died. As she lay on her death-bed,

---

8   Howitt was mistaken in thinking that the sheath was hollow, though perhaps he was only meaning the hole at the top.

she said to her husband, 'Laury, promise me ya thing,—at tou'ill not wed again when I'se gane.' 'Peggy, my lass,' answered Laurence, 'do not mak me promise nae sic thing; tou knaws I'se but young yet.' The old fellow did wed again, and his brother, on returning from the wedding, made this report of the bride:—'Why-a, she's a rough ane. I'se welded owre and owre, an' I canna find a lock o' leggin in her; she's a' footing.'

The neighbouring dale, Garsdale, which is a narrower and more secluded one than Dent, is a great knitting dale. The old men sit there in companies round the fire; and so intent are they on their occupation and stories, that they pin cloths on their shins to prevent them being burnt; and sometimes they may be seen on a bench at the house-front, and where they have come out to cool themselves, sitting in a row knitting with their shin-cloths on, making the oddest appearance imaginable.'

Garsdale was the birthplace in 1734 of Dr. John Dawson, the famous mathematician who was in turn apothecary, surgeon, and teacher of mathematics. In his day he taught eleven Senior Wranglers. As a boy, the son of a farmer, he tended the sheep on the fells, and at night like the rest of the children of that generation he knitted stockings. John was allowed to spend his 'knitting-brass' as he wished, and with it he bought books which started him on his career.

At the end of the last century a character of these dales was old Mally Gibson 'who with coal-scuttle bonnet, faultless cap-border, bare arms and the homeliest of frocks, recalled a bygone age of rural simplicity, as thus equiped she rattled her needles and danced her cop of bump-garn beside her the livelong day.'[9]

In Dentdale now there are certainly no men and very few women who can knit in the old way. It was the elderly people who knitted to the last; and with them have gone almost but not quite all memories of the centuries-old industry. In 1948 we talked to Mr. Burton who is ninety-five, and who for fifty years lived at the Sportsman's Arms near his present home at the head of Dentdale. When he was a little lad, before Cowgill school was built, he was sent every day to the cottage of an old woman who taught two or three of the children a few simple spellings and also how to knit. 'I think they sent us to get us out of the way,' he said with a smile. He himself was never able to knit with the swaying motion, though his womenfolk could. They had to

---

9 *Sedbergh, Garsdale and Dent.* W. Thompson.

The Terrible Knitters e' Dent

walk all the way to Dent Town with the finished garments which were taken to Kendal in a covered cart. The bump was disliked because it was sticky. He remembers that between 1870 and 1875 when the navvies were building the viaducts and line for the Settle-Carlisle Railway which crosses the fells near by, they were taught to knit in their spare time. A Quaker lady who wished to show kindness to the homeless men gave them the lessons. He also spoke of a spinning mill which used to stand beside the Dee below Cowgill Chapel. Here a coarse cloth was made, and yarn was spun for the knitters. Only the foundation stones remain. He remembers too the days when Dent Town was of much greater importance than Sedbergh, when it was not only the post-town, but also the polling centre.

Rash Mill, now a joiner's shop, four miles below Dent Town, was built on or near the site of an ancient manorial corn mill. A deed of 1799 mentions this 'new erected Carding and Spinning Mill' then in the possession of John Bradley, but early in the next century it reverted to corn.

Up Flintergill in Dent where the beck tumbles down a rocky gill in a series of miniature falls, close by the water is a house which a hundred years ago was a weaving-shed. When we visited it, Mrs. Crabtree who lives there came out to meet us, and left behind on the sofa a half-finished sock, and her leather belt and knitting stick. The room she invited us into used to have four looms standing in each corner under windows. Her mother once worked there; and she could remember a little of the old carding song 'Tarry Woo.' There is still an air of companionship lingering in that room which will never feel empty.

Mrs. Crabtree, who is seventy-nine, is one of the very few people who can still knit in the old way. This in Dent is called 'swaving,' meaning the up and down motion of the arms and body. We were shown how to do it; but it was not easy even to see the loops as they slipped from one needle to another. When we complimented her on the speed of her knitting, she only shook her head, and said that she was always one of the lazy ones, but that 'My mother's needles fair made music.' As children they were given so much knitting to do in a day. She told us that her sister always finished hers before breakfast, and was usually two days' work ahead, whilst she herself was often two days behind.

One Christmas Day the children had been promised that as a treat they might go sliding; but she had not finished the allotted amount of knitting, and was told that she must stay at home until it was done. But her father seeing the child said, 'Nay Sally, I'll not have you sittin' knittin' on Kessmas Day. I'll finish it myself.' This he did, so that she was able to go out and play. He also made one of her three knitting sticks and when he gave it to her said that if she did not marry she would still be all right.

Mrs. Crabtree remembers that her mother could knit a jersey or frock, as they were called, in a day, and was paid a shilling for it. Some of the jerseys had a diamond at either side of the front in 'hit and miss it' (one plain, one purl), some were in cable stitch, and others had a square of ribbed knitting from the neck downwards gradually decreasing into a V. They received better payment for the jerseys in fancy stitches. The children often helped their mother by knitting the sleeves of the plain jerseys. Opposite page 53 is a photograph of Mrs. Crabtree's sister bringing home the cops of yarn from the knitting 'shop.' There were two 'shops' in Dent, one for a Kendal firm (perhaps H. Waddington & Co.) and the other for J. Dover & Son, Farfield Mill, Sedbergh. The family had a winder called a 'windle' which at one time was used for winding the homespun yarn into 'clues,' (balls). It consisted of a 'coppy' (stool) with a hole in the middle, and into this was inserted a rod with four arms from which the wool was wound.

We were shown many old photographs, and pieces of china full of precious memories. One, in particular, was a tiny black Wedgwood teapot, of the kind that was used when tea was very scarce—tea that was a luxury, often bought on the proceeds of the knitting. When the time came for us to go, she came to the door and waved good-bye. We shall always think of her as a link with the past—a daughter of a 'terrible knitter e' Dent.'

The knitting sheaths, though often carved and given as presents by young men to their girls or by fathers to their daughters, were sometimes turned out for sale. A few years ago, there lived in Dent, Tubber Pickthall, an old man who made tubs, clothes props, and pegs as well as knitting sheaths which he sold for a few coppers. We have also been told that the tune of the hymn 'Dentdale,' number 804 in the Methodist Hymn Book, is the original air of one of the knitting songs. It is said too—though with what truth we cannot be sure—that the people knitted on their way to church, and that the parson began the service by saying, 'Put down your pricks, we're going to pray.'

Of the patterned gloves described in chapter three, five pairs are from Dentdale. They are all of this century, and were knitted for sale to private individuals, often members of the parties who came to the dale for the grouse shooting. They are no longer made in the valley, and were a last flowering of the art of the old knitters—those people to whom skill in the craft was a birthright from past generations.

Hebblethwaite Hall

CHAPTER VIII
THE ROMANCE OF
HEBBLETHWAITE HALL

AT the foot of the Howgill Hills the market-town of Sedbergh lies, six miles from Dent Town, and eleven from Kendal. With its busy main street, well-stocked shops, and large Public School it is proud of its prosperity and can look forward to the future with assurance; whilst only two and a half miles away situated in a lonely gill is a ruined mill, symbol of industrial pioneers upon whom much of the population once depended for its livelihood.

The information contained in the following pages is largely based on what was probably one of the first ledgers of this early woollen mill. The unique feature about this book is that not only both mill and private accounts dating from 1792 are kept in its pages, but it was also used as a record book for the outgoing mill correspondence between the years 1819 and 1835. We have seen the knitters toiling over the work in their homes, but here to complete our picture we learn of the worries, decisions, necessary gambles, irritations, and day-to-day troubles of the mill-owner—the direct descendant of the old hosier.

Hebblethwaite Hall Woollen Mill was started by a Quaker named Robert Foster. He was born at Lancaster in 1754, was at school at Sedbergh, and being a high-spirited and adventurous youth at the age of eighteen went to Sea. After making three voyages to the West Indies, he was appointed store-keeper in Antigua by his grandfather and great-uncle, Miles and James Birket, who were West India merchants. But he soon returned to sea to fight the privateers in the American War of Independence. These warlike actions were disapproved of by his relatives, and once, when on leave, he scandalised the members of the Quaker community by 'appearing at Brigflatts Meeting House, with his lace cocked hat on his head and a cutlass by his side!'[1] He left the navy about 1779, and took up the management of his grandfather's estate at Hebblethwaite which he inherited in 1785. In 1784 he married Mary Burton, and their eldest son, Miles, was the father of Birket Foster the artist.[2] The prosperous Quaker families, manufacturers, bankers and merchants, in different parts of Yorkshire, Westmorland, and Lancashire frequently intermarried and formed a community of their own. We read of George Birkbeck of Settle lodging with his kinsman, Robert Foster, while he was being coached by John Dawson the Garsdale mathematician. In later life George Birkbeck founded the first Mechanic's Institute.

Robert Foster built the mill about 1792, near the site of a corn mill mentioned in a deed of 1592, 'for the better employment of the poor, established a school for their education, and became a mixture of father, physician, lawyer and judge amongst his dependants.' The ledger records a partnership with a Charles Holme dissolved in 1793, so that the mill probably was started by the two men. The Rev. W. Thompson in his *Sedbergh, Garsdale and Dent* (1892) says that about the year 1794 Miles, the son of Robert Foster, entered into partnership with Joseph Dover who after Miles Foster's death built Farfield Mill, Sedbergh. This partnership is not confirmed by the ledger as Miles Foster's name is never mentioned, and the letters dating from 1819 are signed Joseph Dover and after 1828 Joseph Dover & Son. We do know that in 1812 Robert Foster retired to live in Newcastle and died in 1827.

---

1 *A Memorial of Cowgill Chapel*. Adam Sedgwick.
2 *Birket Foster*. H. M. Cundall.

The estate was sold by auction in September 1812. A sale bill which has been preserved gives the following particulars:

HEBLETHWAITE HALL;

Comprising the Mansion-House, a good Farmhouse, and outbuildings; also MILLS, and other conveniences now used in, and well adapted for, carrying on the Woollen Manufacture; and about three hundred Acres of very improvable Arable, Meadow, Pasture, and Wood Land, Within a Ring-fence, the Land Tax whereof is redeemed and enjoying various Rents Boons, and other Seignorial Rights.

This estate adjoins the Turn-pike road leading through the market-town of Sedbergh from Brough to Kendal, and is distant about 12 miles from the latter place. The lands command a good view of the vale of Sedbergh, are well wooded and stocked with game, and the streams therein and in the neighbourhood abound with Trout.

On the back of the sale bill is a note, signed by Robert Foster, the owner, to say that he has appointed Anthony Clapham of Newcastle to bid at and purchase any part of the Estates for R. Foster's own use. However, on February 12th, 1813, the whole estate, including the mills and three cottages and also Sarthwaite Farm, was transferred by deed from Robert Foster to Warwick Pearson for £10,800. The wood consisting of oak and other timber trees was of great value.

Joseph Dover, who certainly rented and ran the mill after 1812 is the main figure in its story. The Dovers belonged to Keswick where some of the family were woollen manufacturers and others farmers; and Joseph may have come first to Hebblethwaite as manager. He did not own the estate himself as in a letter of 1822 he spoke of hard times which had forced his landlord, Warwick Pearson, to sell some of his farms. He spoke also of a personal tragedy when in March, 1824, three of his children died of a fever from which the whole family had suffered. Joseph Dover was a downright character and an astute business man. Under him trade increased, and needing more room for expansion he built Farfield Mill, Sedbergh in 1837, the year before he died. Hebblethwaite Mill was left, and became a bobbin and saw-mill. It eventually fell into ruin, and its stones were carted away for other uses.

Before turning the pages of the ledger let us journey to Hebblethwaite Hall and take a look at the ruins of the mill in which so much work was done; where yarn was spun both for cloth and for knitting and the garments put through finishing processes; and from where all the goods had to be carried by cart. About two miles out of Sedbergh on the Kirkby Stephen road we leave the broad backs of the Howgill Hills behind us, and turn up an inconspicuous lane which runs uphill between fields. The way gradually narrows, high banks topped with hedges close in on either hand, ruts and loose stones become more numerous, until after about half a mile round a corner and guarded by fine sycamores, two farms and a cottage come into view. The farm-house on the right is Hebblethwaite Hall. It is a large house built in the early Georgian period, with a wide oak staircase and panelled cupboards in its thick walls, but otherwise with no outstanding architectural features.

From the close-cropped pasture behind the house the great bulk of Baugh Fell dominates and fills the skyline. Over to the right a deep belt of beeches grows in profusion down a steep hillside. These mossy slopes form one side of the cradle of a little peaty stream far below, upon whose surface the sunshine filters fitfully through the leafy network overhead. A green track leads us purposefully downwards, but even with this for guidance it is easy to miss the few remnants of what was once a centre of industry. Just below where a waterfall pours a spout of milky foam into a pool, are the lower courses of two buildings which once stood close to the water's edge. Trees are growing out of the ruins; thick moss and harts' tongue fern hang from crevices in the stonework; cranesbill and nettles flourish abundantly, and water trickles in a bed of yellow slime down the corner of a building. Old gooseberry bushes shoot up from the damp earth, surely once part of the garden of a cottage that is said to have existed near by. We think of Nanny Atkinson, a wool-sorter, who one morning was found dead in the gill, down which she had fallen in the dark. From such gloom and silence it is good to regain the track and follow the way used by the mill carts, round below the house to where it rejoins the lane near the sycamores. One of the fields where the cloth was hung out to dry is still called the tenter field.

The ledger which we are about to open is a long thick book bound in vellum. On the outside are printed by hand 'R. F. LEDGER,' and above is written 'John Dover Heblethwaite Hall Waste Book.' Accounts between the years 1792 and 1795 are kept at each end of the book and in between are the letters, many of which are quoted in an appendix on page 104 [see Appendix E, page 119, in this edition]. The debit and credit accounts are headed SPINNING ROOM Account, BUMP Account, accounts of the deliveries of knitted goods such as HOSE, Bonts (bonnets), Du caps (Dutch caps—like sun-bonnets), KILMK CAPS (Kilmarnock caps in shape like a tam o' shanter), CHARITY CAPS

(caps dyed blue, black & green worn with a ribbon tied under the chin, for children in charity schools), MITTS and GLOVES. There is an account with George Braithwaite of Kendal for manufactured goods and bump. Other pages are devoted to accounts of yarn stockings, oil, dyers, linseys, carding-engine, factory, mill, and personal accounts headed with a name, for instance, Robert Foster. Items are given of business done with places far apart, with wholesalers in London, and drapers of Stockton, Newcastle, Gateshead, Barnard Castle, Appleby, Penrith, Carlisle, Kendal, Ravenstonedale, Kirkby Stephen, Dent, Bishopdale, Lancaster, and Liverpool. The bankers were John Wakefield & Son of Kendal.

Several pages give details of wool bought from Cumberland with remarks at one side such as:—'knitting wool, secd white, short, 10lb alowd for wet, cors skin, skin fine gray, fine skin, noyles, Head wool, Broad Head, Head gray, ointed wool, fine stricken, a bag of picklock, half bread wool, fleece wool, and scotch shorts.'

John Turrel of Brackenthwaite near Crummock Water was a family friend who acted as agent for Joseph Dover in his transactions with the Cumberland statesmen. There are some excellent letters written to him on business and personal matters which show the state of farming and of trade in the county in general. A John Betham acted in the same capacity in London between the mill and the wholesale merchants. He was the recipient of presents from the Dovers such as hams and potted trout.

Reading between the lines we sense the busy days in June when the sheep gathered together from the craggy mountains were driven down for the clippings, and the storing of the fleeces in the wool rooms by the astute farmers who waited for a good price for their clips. On his part Joseph Dover waited too for the moment when the market was in his favour. But he was always anxious to buy Herdwick wool from Cumberland—a finer wool than that of the Blackfaced sheep. Each individual farmer had a reputation for good or bad clips, and those from Newlands and Buttermere were the most highly prized.

After a bargain had been made the wool was taken in packs of eighteen or twenty stones to a warehouse such as those of J. Robinson at Keswick and Cockermouth. From there it was collected by carriers, one being Taylor of Sedbergh, who brought it to Hebblethwaite. On arrival the wool was opened out and weighed; complaints were filed immediately if the weight was wrong—often owing to wet wool—or if it was in bad condition. An Act of

Parliament of 1788 protected the buyers against the fraudulent inclusion of loose wool, dirt etc., in the rolled-up fleeces.

Most processes were carried through in the mill except dyeing, the knitting, and the weaving. The machinery was the same as that described in Low Mill, Askrigg. Weaving took place on the hand-looms at Weavers' Yard in Sedbergh. Here were woven Kerseys, a narrow coarse cloth called after the place of that name in Suffolk; sagathy, a kind of serge used for aprons; and checks and plaidings used for horse collars and rugs. These were then returned to the mill to be fulled and washed.

Suitable knitting yarn was given out to the knitters of the district, and a cart travelled once a week to Dent to carry wool and to collect the finished garments. Even then the older people were spoken of as the best knitters as if the younger ones were becoming less skilled in the craft. The knitted articles were fulled (milled) having been made large to allow for shrinkage.

The goods sent to London were taken by carrier over Stainmore to Stockton from where they went by sea; or by carrier to Lancaster and thence by canal to London. The firm had a year's contract with a John Benson who agreed to transport goods to Stockton at a rate of 2/4d. per cwt., and to Newcastle at 3/1d. per cwt. Their largest customer in London for a long period was John Kynaston of Gutter Lane. Over a few months the account with this house was as much as £1,000. From this tiny mill very large orders were sent out. One of the last letters quoted from the ledger records the acceptance of an order for 3,000 dozen Kilmarnock caps at 4/– a dozen. One of the most interesting customers of Hebblethwaite Hall Mill was the firm of I. & R. Morley, founded in 1795, today one of the largest firms of hosiery manufacturers in the country. The address given in the ledger will still find one of the head offices of the company.

The Romance of Hebblethwaite Hall

It is interesting to note the fluctuations in the prices of wool and their effect on the cloth and garments sold. The following table gives some idea of this:—

Year	Paid for Cumberland Wool per Stone (17 lbs)	Paid for Local Wool Per st. (17 lbs)	Wholesale Price of White Kerseys Per yard	Blue Bonts.	Black Bonts.	Green Bonts.
				Wholesale price Per dozen		
1819	13/-	—	20d	9/6	—	—
1820	9/- 9/6	—	20d	—	7/3	8/3
1821	11/6 12/-	8/9 9/6	15d 16½d	—	6/9	—
1822	7/- 7/3	6/6 7/-	15d	7/6	6/6	7/6
1823	6/- 7/6	4/6 (coarse)	13½d	—	—	—
1824	7/6 8/3 8/4	9/- (?)	12½d 13d	7/3	6/3	7/3
1825	10/3 11/- 12/-	10/- 10/6	15d 17d 18d	—	—	—
1826	7/- 7/6	5/- 5/6	12d 12½d 13d	7/3	6/3	7/-

The second and third prices given show the rise in value during the same year.

The letters mention such varied subjects as the cost and description of machinery, the runs on small banks throughout the country, remarks about the hay and corn harvests, and the fairs at Yarm and Brough Hill. Others show up the troubles of Poor Law relief in the bands of the overseers of the parishes. Seen against the background of the times the items of local news contained in these letters take on a wider significance. The mentions of bad years and the disturbed state of the countryside remind us that the Napoleonic Wars had only just ended. There was also much misery amongst the poor created by the rise in the price of bread due to the Corn Law of 1815, and these facts combined with the growing demand for Parliamentary Reform accounted for much of the unrest up and down the land.

There is one letter of November 23rd, 1826 [see page 133] which gives a unique description of the method of making Kilmarnock caps. For these the knitter used nine pairs of needles. A few other letters remark upon the work done by the best knitters, and the difficulty of getting them to knit 'frocks' because it was such heavy work. These frocks, sometimes called jackets, were large sailors' Guernseys of different qualities and weights, some with roll collars and some with open necks. There are also spotted frocks speckled with another colour, already mentioned in the third chapter.

Joseph Dover makes careful enquiries as to whether a new customer is a fit person for the allowance of credit. He has no use for those who do not pay their bills punctually. A letter written in 1825 ends: 'I therefore request you will remit me by return without fail otherwise hostile measures will be resorted to.' In the early letters which Joseph Dover appears to have written himself, there is very little attempt at punctuation and the spelling is delightfully odd; but later when his son John becomes a partner in the business and deals with the correspondence, the spelling and phrasing become more conventional. They both use the long 'f' for 's' throughout. A list of some of the people mentioned in the letters and the accounts will be found in the appendix, but this is incomplete as the addresses were not always given; and the answering letters were not preserved. A list of employees at Hebblethwaite Hall Mill is also added.

When the firm moved to the new mill, Farfield, on the river Clough near Sedbergh, John Dover carried on the business. Later his brother James bought Millthrop Mill on the river Rawthey south of the town. This and Birks Mill a mile away were built as cotton mills early in the nineteenth century, and as late as 1848 were both being run for that purpose by James Upton and Son. At Millthrop the manufacture of horse collar checks was started, and continued until the mill closed in 1931. Birks which at one time was a bobbin mill and dyehouse was eventually bought by the Dovers of Farfield for spinning yarn. In the neighbourhood was a third mill at Howgill up the valley of the Lune. This was in 1838 run by a W. G. Best, woollen manufacturer.

At Farfield with its larger premises and better accessibility trade took on a new impetus. A small hamlet, Hall Bank, on the Garsdale road grew up to house the workers, and later large Victorian houses for the Dovers themselves were built nearby. They gradually bought up neighbouring farms, for which the tenants paid rent with their wool clips. In later days the kerseys were woven from Australian wool, and exported to Australia to be used as horse cloths. Checked cloth made from local wool was sold as linings for horse-collars; a few blankets were manufactured and sold in pairs here and there. The firm supplied horse-cloths for Queen Victoria and Edward VII. For the Queen they had to be specially made and always in quiet colours. We have been shown a length of kersey dyed dark blue with red checks, and a piece of lining, white with red checks; both, made from pure wool, felt as though they would wear for ever. But unfortunately we have been unable to trace any knitted garments.

The Romance of Hebblethwaite Hall

The knitting trade still went on; the firm practically had a monopoly in miners' garments sent to Newcastle. The covered carts not only journeyed to Dent and Garsdale with the knitting wool, but over into the North Riding to Hawes to deliver wool for the knitters. These people, home-employees of the mill, delighted to send back with the carter little notes asking for more wool. A heap of them was kept on a file in the office until 1937.

When the goods were brought back to the mill, they were weighed to check over the amount of wool used. The knitted caps and stockings were then milled; and the caps stretched on round boards, and the stockings on leg-boards. The frocks were not milled, and were occasionally dyed blue. The white ones were washed and stoved in sulphur fumes, and finally they were done up in parcels of a quarter of a dozen. About 1890 knitting machines were installed; and girls were employed to work them, though women finished the garments at home by sewing up the seams and putting in the sleeves. The hand-knitting continued side by side with the machine-knitting until the first years of the present century when it ceased.

In 1909 Farfield Mill was burnt down, but this disaster proved providential as it was built up again on modern lines. In common with many other firms the Dover's cloth trade received a severe set-back when Australia introduced tariffs for imported cloth, and this together with the decreasing use of horses caused them to sell the mill in 1937. It was bought by the Farfield Spinning Co. for the manufacture of carpet yarn. In 1940 it was requisitioned by the government for Armstrong Siddeleys, and later was used as an Admiralty stores. But in 1947 it was released, and handed back to the Spinning Company.

Though the mill is now driven by electricity and the modern carding engines run more evenly and faster than those driven by water-power, much of the old life remains. Descendants of families who generation after generation were employed by the Dovers still work there. New Zealand wool with its soft handle and lustre is used for some carpet yarn, but Cumberland, Yorkshire and Westmorland wool is purchased for other qualities; though now, due to the wool control, it cannot be bought direct from the farmers as in the old days.

With the story of Hebblethwaite and Farfield Mills we have reached the end of our search. By following the fast-vanishing tracks which they left behind, for a brief period, the old hand-knitters have regained their importance. As we pored over the ledgers and old documents, or sat talking around the firesides of many a dales' home, and were shown a faded photograph here, a treasured knitting sheath there, little pieces of the jig-saw came into our hands; until the picture gradually began to form and at last each bit fell into its rightful place. But the inanimate objects alone could not have led us far were it nor for the kindly folk who have breathed life into them.

APPENDICES

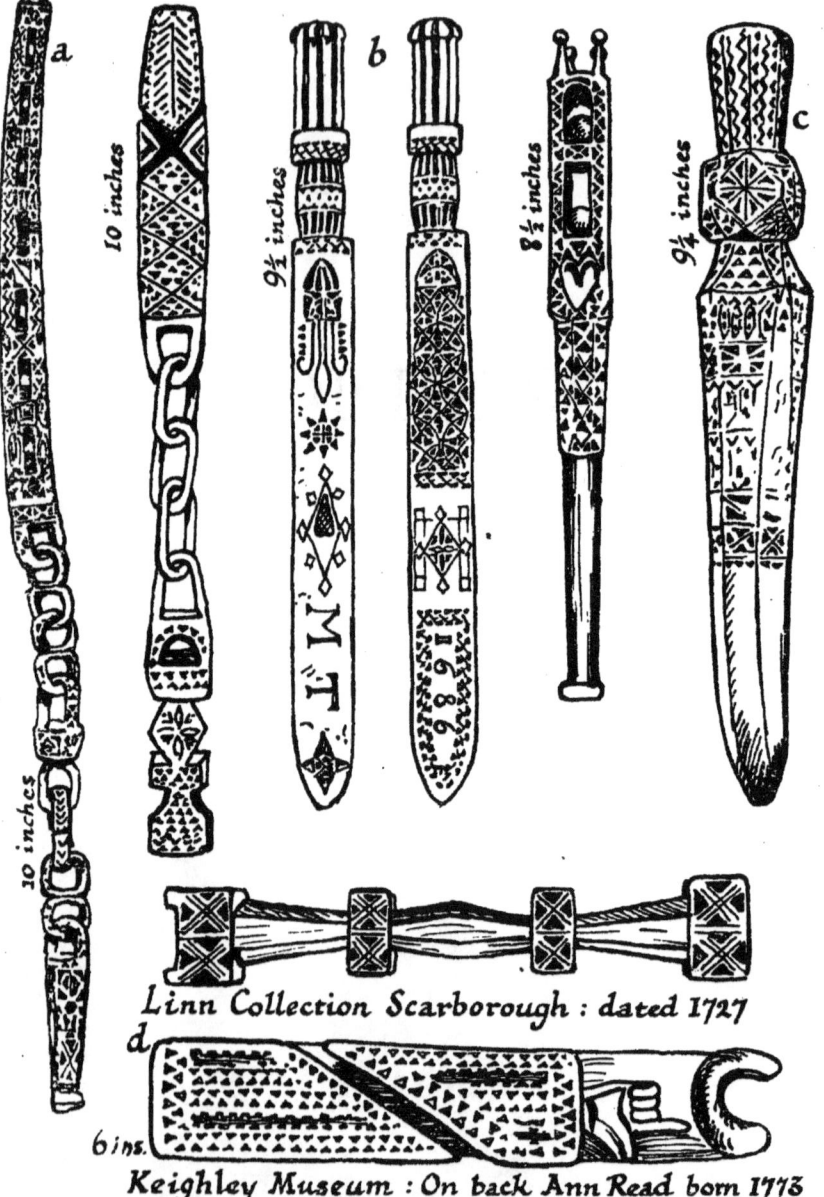

Appendix A

Knitting Sheaths

FROM the first introduction of knitting into England, it is probable that some form of holder to support the needle was used. But of all the thousands of wooden knitting sheaths, or sticks as they may be called, employed throughout the centuries, comparatively few have survived, and of these only one of an early date is recorded. This isolated example is described in detail by O. Evan-Thomas in Domestic Utensils of Wood. The writer suggests that it may be fifteenth century and of Scandinavian or Northumbrian origin. It is a rectangular piece of boxwood or fruitwood, 9¾ inches long and ¾ wide, sculptured in high relief with little scenes, such as priests praying, a dog baiting a bull, and a bear chained to a church porch. Bear-baiting reached a climax as a common sport in Elizabethan times. This together with the fact that knitting flourished then as never before, suggests that the sixteenth century is a more probable date. Also, knitting was not known so early in Scandinavia, and as the carvings show no real affinity to early Northumbrian art, we would suggest an origin in one of the early knitting centres.

Though the sheaths are seldom dated, many are adorned with initials and elaborate chip-carving. Hearts often form a motive in the design. Like the Welsh love-spoons, stay-busks, and lace-bobbins, they were embellished and given as love-tokens by young men to their sweethearts. Many, indeed, show the innate good taste of their carvers, and can be regarded as forming a small branch of peasant art. Almost every kind of wood was used from fruitwood—often taken from a favourite tree in a countryman's orchard—to wood of forest trees such as oak, beech, and sycamore, and in later days, cedar and mahogany. They were also made for sale by country craftsmen, therefore occasionally two are found alike. Others fashioned for pure use from any available bit of wood, such as an old door, are clumsy and plain, and often these are the most well-worn. Some have a ledge or slit so that they can be held firmly in the belt or apron-string.

Treasured as keepsakes many knitting sticks are yet to be found dales' homes. When people handle them a far away look comes into their eyes. They

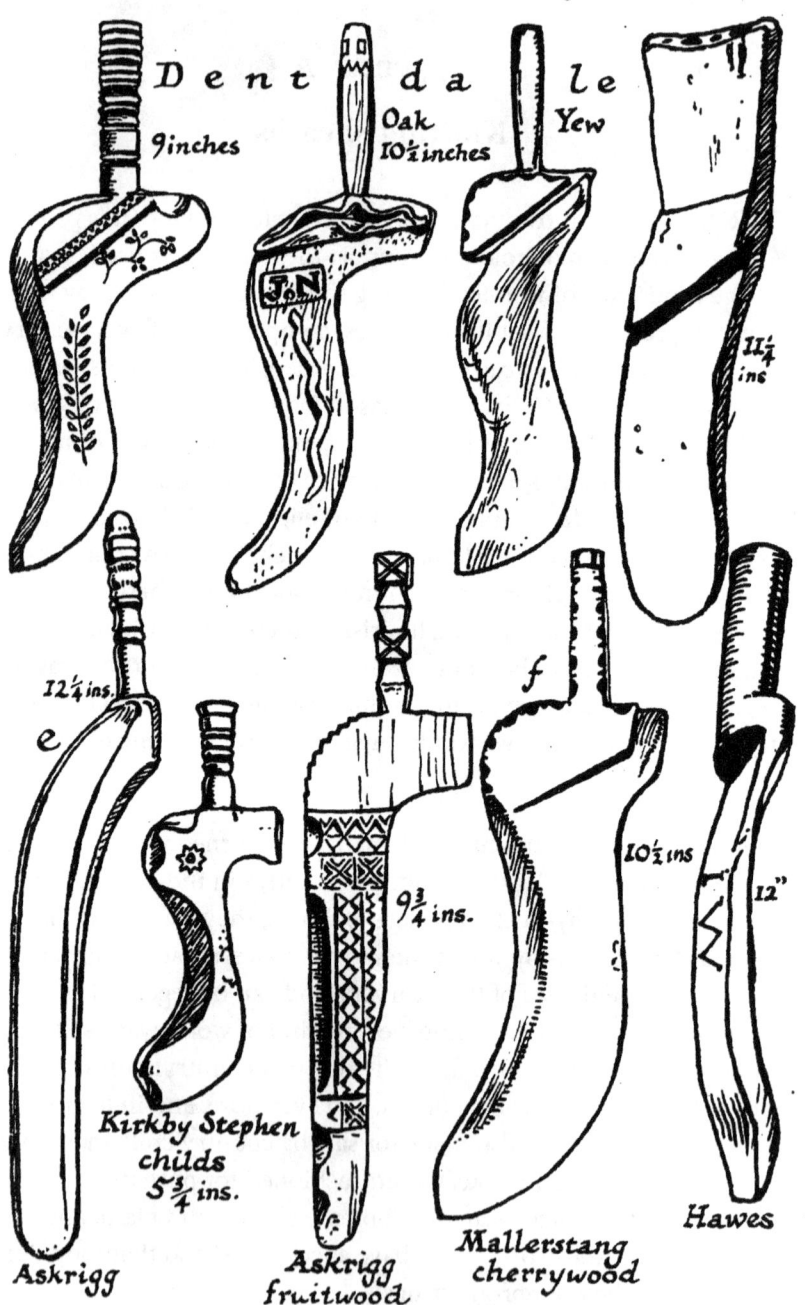

Appendix A

remember stories told by their parents of the days of long ago. 'Aye, that was given to my mother by a lad who was drowned,' said a friend of ours. 'He was on horseback driving some sheep across the Eden in Mallerstang. The horse and sheep got over safely, but he was swept away by the flooded river.' Of another we have been told: 'This belonged to the mother of a dear old friend who gave it to me. She was born in 1823 and died in 1900. She could neither read nor write, and was never in a train in her life. Old Nanny was a fine, intelligent character, and in spite of her illiteracy made out her own bills by chalk-marks on her kitchen door.' Figures e and f show the sheaths which belonged to these two people.

The regional variety of the Yorkshire and Westmorland dales is shaped like a goose's wing. We have only seen one from Swaledale that was straight and rectangular. Very few of those remaining in the dales are elaborately carved, but most have some adornment. The haft often has a bone or metal cap to prevent the hole in the wood at the top from being worn too large by the movement of the needle.

The Yorkshire museums, in particular Halifax, Scarborough, and Keighley, and several private collectors have numbers of knitting sheaths.[1] Through the years many of these have changed hands so often that it is difficult to trace the place of their origin. Dated 1686 the earliest example that we have seen is at the Bankfield Museum, Halifax (Figure b). This is of great interest as it is known to have been bought at Wimborne in Dorset, one of the important knitting centres in the seventeenth century. Two others of this era are recorded by W. Ruskin Butterfield in the *Connoisseur* (1919).

Considerably more knitting sheaths are preserved from the eighteenth century, and several are dated. To this period can be ascribed with certainty those with fine and complicated chip-carving. This art degenerated into formless designs, whereas the older examples all had well-arranged geometric patterns. Different areas developed different styles. One early recognisable type is spatula-shaped with a many faceted block of wood at the base of the haft (Figure c). A later eighteenth-century variety has loose balls carved in open cages. A particularly delicate knitting stick from the Bankfield Museum has six balls in six cages (Figure a). This example also includes another form, that is, two sections joined together by a wooden chain—the whole carved from one piece of wood. These have either a hole or a hook at the lower end to

---

1   In the illustrations the knitting sheaths not assigned elsewhere are in our collection.

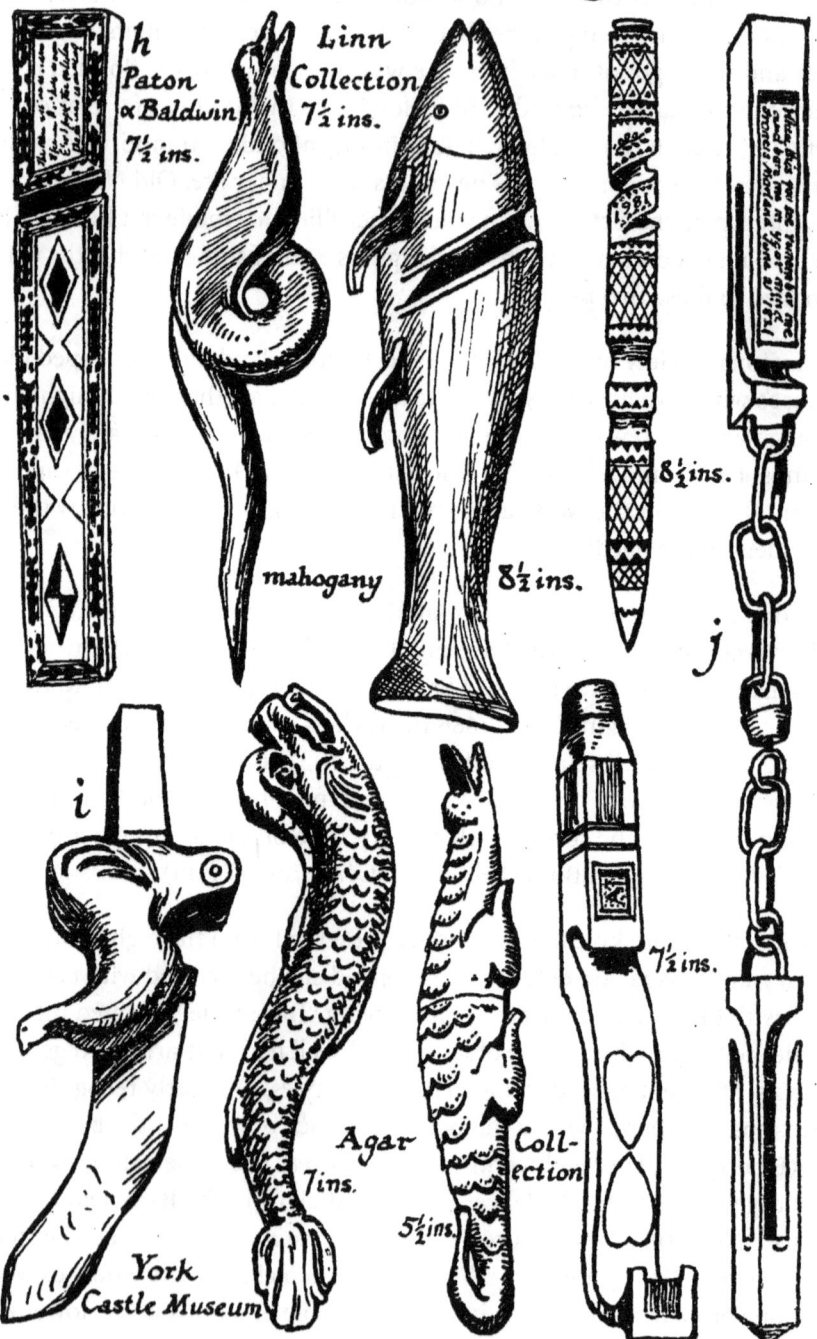

Appendix A

which the ball of wool could be attached, and they went on being made into the nineteenth century (Figure j, dated 1821). The decorations of Welsh lovespoons include both the loose ball and the chain form or ornament.

Some curious motives carved on the knitting sheaths appear to have a symbolic meaning, though not all are decipherable. For example an eighteenth-century stick at Keighley and one at Scarborough, almost identical, show a pointing hand, a token of fidelity. These have six separate holes for the needle bored in the top (Figure d). A third at Scarborough has inset a red heart on a black hand made of a tarry substance. This is a Holy seal of the sacred hand and heart, symbol of faithfulness between two lovers, evolved like the bridal garters in the north-east moorlands of Yorkshire. An early goose-wing shaped variety has incised on it a rising sun, a cock, and other devices, perhaps of religious significance (Figure l).

By far the greatest number of knitting sheaths that have survived are of nineteenth century date. Some of our particular dales' type—the goosewing—are without doubt late eighteenth century, but most are last century, and the earliest dated example is 1780. They were widely used in the north of England, and also in Wales.

A very different but well-defined group, of which we have seen fourteen examples, mostly in the Linn collection at Scarborough, probably comes from the north-east coast. They are of mahogany, rectangular, slightly curved, sometimes terminating in a scroll, and beautifully inlaid. The earliest specimen we have seen is dated 1828, and has insets of bone in diamond and heart shapes. Others have both bone insets, and borders of inlaid different coloured woods, whilst some instead of bone insets have glass-windows covering written mottoes and the name of the recipient (Figure h). One has Elizabeth Arnett, Seaham Harbour, 1865, written on paper under a glass window. Only a craftsman in the art of inlay could have produced this fine work.

The realistic fish and serpent-shaped knitting sheaths, usually made of mahogany are of a late type. The one adorned with a cock in bold relief has on the back yellow leaves painted on a red ground (Figure i). Besides these are the spindle-shaped sticks commonly used in the industrial West Riding, South Yorkshire, and Wales. Produced by mechanical turning on a lathe, they do not compare in interest with the early carved specimens. A further development of industrial areas, such as Durham, are the metal sheaths, usually of brass. Keighley Museum has a fine collection of these, as well as a

Knitting Sheaths of Various Materials

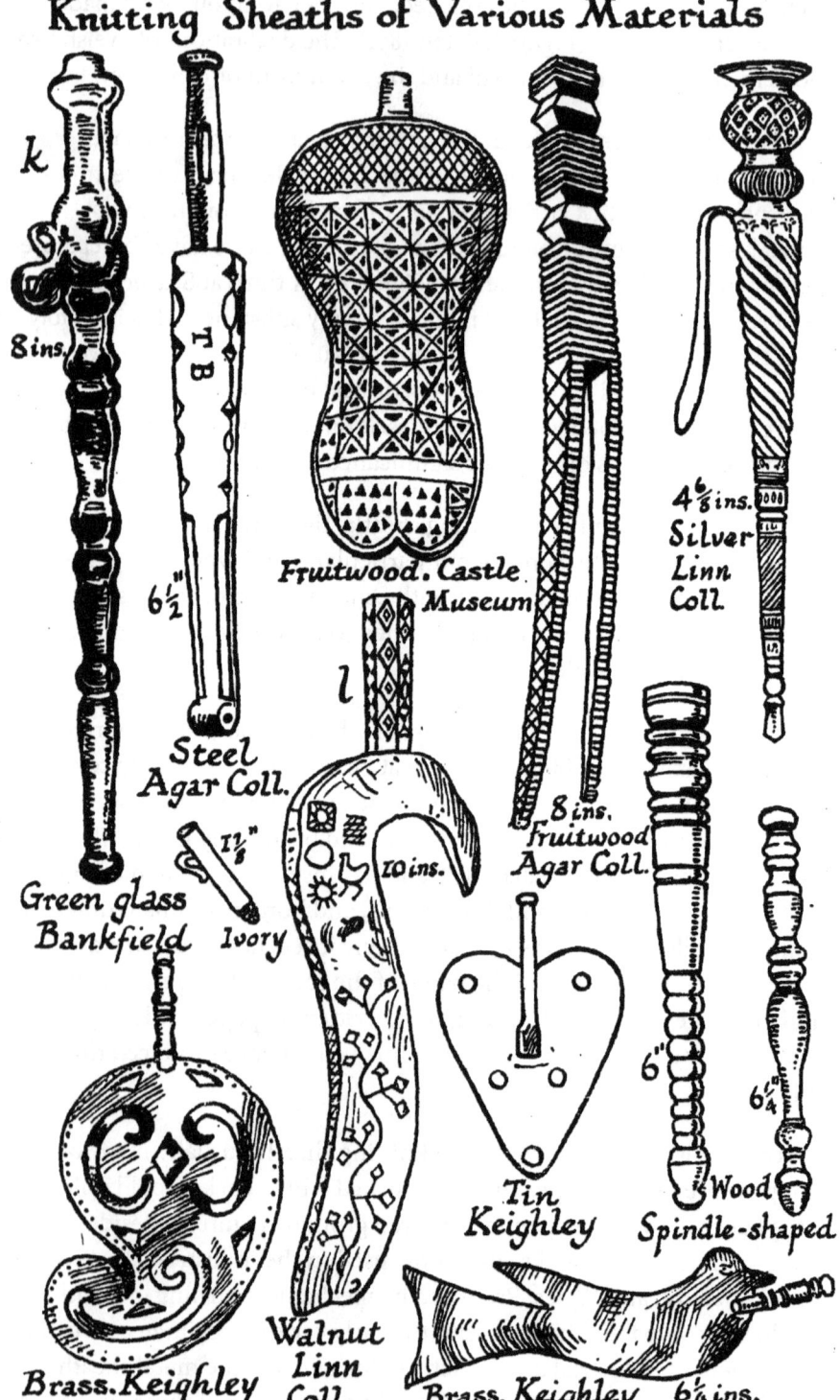

Appendix A

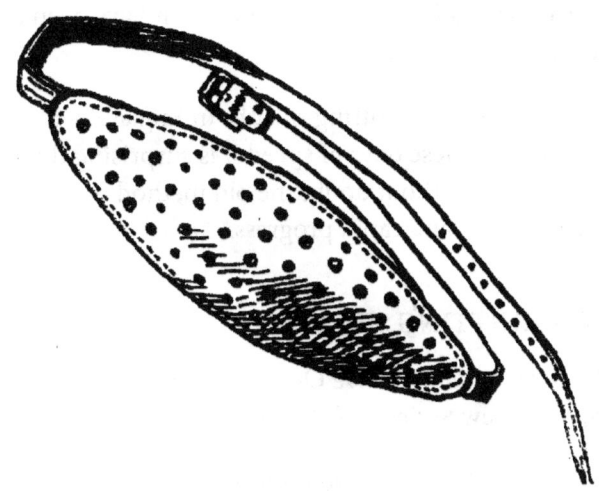

Highland Knitting Pad

heart-shaped tin one pierced round with holes to sew it to the waist-band. Silver, bone, and ivory have all been used for making knitting sticks; and usually the silver ones are Continental. A unique example at the Bankfield Museum is of green glass (Figure k), perhaps dating from when dairy utensils such as bowls were made of thick green glass in the last century; whilst one in the Agar collection is simply a piece of stag's horn, and lastly one is a smooth twig. That the ancient peasant art of carving knitting sheaths survives, is shown by one now in York Castle Museum made by an old man at Rosedale in the north-east moorlands in 1935.

Sometimes ingenuity contrived pads, into which the needle could be stuck, from tight wisps of straw which William Howitt describes in Dentdale. Or in Northumberland bundles of sticks sewn into a linen bag were used, called 'bundley sticks.' There were also the quilted quills dating back to 1770, and used in Westmorland in this century. These consisted of goose quills sewn into a piece of cloth to be pinned on to the knitters' dress. Perhaps some of these simple devices throw a light upon what the dalespeople used before their wooden sheaths.

Though quills are known to have been made into holders in the Shetland Islands, and a wooden stick is recorded from Skaill in Orkney,[2] at the present day the crofters of the Islands and the Highlands of Scotland employ a leather pad stuffed with horse-hair and punched with numerous holes (Figure m).

---

2 For a drawing see *Archaeologia*. Vol. XXXIV, p. 95.

Old Hand-Knitters of the Dales

These are sometimes made by the local sadler, but have been also imported in large numbers from Scandinavia.

In another generation or so knitting sheaths in England will probably only be found in museums. In these days of speed it is surprising that they have not returned to favour, for without doubt the old method of knitting made for efficiency, even tension, and rapid progress.

ARTICLES ON KNITTING SHEATHS

1. *Some Late Survivals of Primitive Ornament*, by J. Romilly Allen. *The Reliquary.* New Series. Vol. IX. 1903.

2. *Knitting Sticks. The Reliquary.* New Series. Vol. X. 1904.

3. Article by R. S. Ferguson. *Journal of British Archaeological Association.* Vol. XXVII.

4. Article by R. S. Ferguson. *Transactions Cumberland & Westmorland Antiquarian Society.* Vol. VI.

5. Article by C. A. Parker. *Transactions Cumberland & Westmorland Antiquarian Society.* Vol. XVII. 1917.

6. *Some Knitting Implements of Cumberland & Westmorland* by J. C. Varty-Smith. *The Connoisseur.* 1909.

7. *About Knitting Sticks* by W. Ruskin Butterfield. *The Connoisseur.* 1919.

8. *Domestic Utensils of Wood.* Owen Evan-Thomas.

9. Mary Thomas's *Knitting Book.* 1938.

10. *The Knitters Craft* by James Walton. *Country Life.* Vol. CII No. 2639. 1947.

Appendix B

List of People Employed Latterly at Hebblethwaite Hall Mill

(Supplied by Mr. J. D. Betham)

Samuel Leighton (spinner).
Tom Allan (spinner) father of Tom Allan who had the small stocking mill at Appleby on Coupland Beck.
John Crawford (walk miller).
Will Thompson (knockabout—odd jobs).
William Ottaway (knockabout).
James Moorhouse (weaver).
Joseph Moorhouse (weaver).
Harry Cunningham (weaver).
Henry Dover (weaver).
Nanny Atkinson (wool sorter).
Robert Handley (weaver).
Danny Mason (bobbin winder).
Thos. Mackereth (knockabout).
William Robinson (knockabout).
John Leighton (feeder).
Ellen Leighton (feeder).
Jane Crawford (bobbin winder).
Mary Crawford.
Thos. Leighton.
Joseph Dover (weaver).
John Handley (knockabout).
Thos. Farrer (warehouseman & carter).

Appendix C

Cumberland Farmers from Whom J. Dover Bought Wool

Clark John, Cragg House, Buttermere. Yeoman.
Cowman J., Buttermere.
Dover Henry, Gill Brow, Newlands, Keswick.
Fearon Isaac, Loweswater. Yeoman.
Fidler John, Newlands, Keswick.
Grisedale Robert, Patterdale.
Harrison Isaac, Keswick district.
Turrel John, Agent for buying wool.

Appendix D
List of Firms Mentioned in Hebblethwaite Hall Ledger

Alderson R., Stone House, Dent.
Atkinson B., Stockton. Draper (?).
Atkinson Jos. & John, Kendal. Wool Dealers.
Atkinson T., Sedbergh.
Bainbridge J., Newcastle. Wholesale Merchants and Drapers.
Bank Jos., Keswick. Shoemaker.
Bannister Dawson, Dent. Worsted and Stocking yarn mfr.
Benson John, Sedbergh. Carrier to Kendal and Hawes.
Betham W. J., 9, Water Lane, Lower Thames St., London. Agent for the London business.
Blenkarn W. J., London. Wholesale Merchant.
Blyth John, Hawes. Knit Hosiery Mfr.
Bonus J., Lower Thames St. London. Wholesale Merchants.
Braithwaite G., Kendal. Woollen Mfr.
Buckley & Kennan, Liverpool. Merchants.
Carr R., Gateshead.
Chapman, Sedbergh. Carrier to Lancaster.
Coser T., Stockton. Draper.
Dent William, Sandspot, Mallerstang.
Dobson Matthew, Leyburn. Attorney.
Dobson Samuel, Gateshead. Draper.
Dobson Thos., Penrith. Draper (?).
Dover Daniel, Applethwaite Under Skiddaw, Keswick. Woollen Mfr.
Eavell & Bousefield, 247, Tooley St., Southwark.
Foster Elizabeth, Lancaster.
Gandy John & Son, Kendal. Dyers.
Gartside A., Liverpool.
Greathead John., Richmond (?).
Hanley Thos., Sedbergh. Draper.
Harrington Wm. & John, Carlisle. Skinners.
Harrison John, Crook Hill, Kendal. Worsted Spinners. (Dyers?).
Hewitson David, Kirkby Stephen. Carrier to Kendal.

Hodgson Thos., Darlington. Draper.
Hudson Thomas, Penrith. Skinner.
Knowles E. A., Haverdale Mill, Low Row. Knit Hosiery Mfr.
Kynaston W. & J. & Son, Gutter Lane, London. Wholesale Merchants.
Morley I. & R., Wood St., London. Wholesale Merchants.
Norman Charles, Parten, Nr. Whitehaven. Tanners.
Oliver R., Newcastle.
Pickfords & Co., Wood St., London. Carriers.
Relph Isaac, Ravenstonedale.
Richardson John, Burton in Bishopdale. Hosier.
Robinson John, High Hill, Under Skiddaw, Keswick. Warehouseman at Keswick & Cockermouth.
Rooking John, Kirkby Stephen.
Sanders John, Keswick.
Smith G., Newcastle.
Spence Mary & Son, Kirkby Stephen. Draper.
Spencer & Brown, Kirkby Stephen. Draper.
Spencer W. & J., 12, Bow Churchyard, London. Wholesale Merchants.
Spottswood, Barnard Castle.
Taylor, Sedbergh. Carrier.
Thistlethwaite Jer., Dent (?).
Thompson John, Hawes. Draper (?).
Wakefield John & Son, Kendal. Bankers.
Wallas R., Sedbergh.
Watson J., Northallerton.
Wilkinson John & Co., Stockton. Wharfingers.
Wilson James, Appleby.
Wilson Thomas, Kendal. Hosier.
Winskill & Co., Barnard Castle. Draper.

Appendix E

Joseph Dover's Letters[1]

(Low prices in the Yorkshire wool trade)

1819 August 4
Mr John Turrel
   Dear Friend
        It is now som time since any letters has past betwixt you & me I should like to know by Return of post of how wool is likely to Sell with you this year and if their is any Sold and what the prices is likely to be I intend to com over into your part but as yet I cannot tell when it will be the wool trade in Yorkshire is verey bad and there has been verey little Sold Since the Clip and that was Sold at less then half the price that it gave the last year please to give my Respects to your Father & Mother and all your friends
     I remain
       your most obedt.
         Joseph Dover

(A complaint to the carrier)

1819
Nov 20t
Mr Davd Hewetson
   Sir
       I of late had frequent complents of goods Sent off that they have been detained on the rode and one truss of late for Mr Saml Dobson Gateshead which was Sent of on the 1t Novr he wrote me on the 13 Inst that it was not got to hand I wish that you would let me Know by return when that truss was delivered if I cannot have them mor regular don I must send them by som other carrier
        J Dover

---

1 The sentence in brackets above each letter describes the contents.

(Instructions to the agent to buy wool from the Cumberland farmers)

1819
Novr 26t
Mr John Turrel
        Dear Friend

I have Recd your letter of the 22d Inst. With account of the Wool now I shall want a fewe packs more of wool if you can buy me 8 or 10 packs not above 12/shillings p ston. I wish you would do it if Thos Stentons wool is good you may buy it and Jonathan Achison but he is such a werey man in weight but if you buy it you must manage him as well as you can—or you can buy any other Stocks of wool if you find it good now if you could buy Isaac Harrisons wool it would be as much as I should want you may give him 12/6 and if he give you a faire weight of it Sooner than live it you may give him 12/9 pr Stone you bid again at it, you then can buy where you find it good you please to let me know as soon as you can what you get don and what sheets will be wanted I don not Know that I can com my Self but what you buy I shall Remit you money to take it up with and Same time the ballance of cash that is Due to you for your attention and I shall please you for it please give my Respects to all your friends
        I remain your most obdt
                J. Dover

(Directions for packing wool. From a letter to John Turrel headed Heblethwaite Hall Dec. 15th, 1819)

When you go to pack you must call on old John Clark and give my respects to him and Say that I disire he will go with you and lend you a hand at either weing or packing I expect Isac Harrison will give you fair weight as the price is high you can put in to a sheet 18 or 20 ston and to have a packing fleece at everey 16 ston you must take the No. of fleeces in each sheet as well as the weight if Isac Harrison wool be lying where we looked at it.

    I rather think that it will be dampy at the bottom and the walles but that mater you must look to if it be so he must alowe for it he must deliver his wool at Keswick and, take the No of the sheets I expect Isaac Harrison will give you somthing hansom again out of 13/- per stone it is the highest price that I have given for any wool this year pleas to give my Respects to all your friends
        I remain your most ob
                Jos Dover

Appendix E

(Bad weather and tenters)

Heblethwaite Hall
Dec 20 1819
Mr Saml Dobson
        Sir
                I have received your letter I have none of the 3/4 red checks made but I can make you 2/ps but now the weather is so uncertain for getting them dryed of that I cannot State any time it may be 4 or 5 weeks as we sum times at this season of the year cannot get any good dryd of the tenters for many weeks, and the white Kersey and plaidings we have none of them upon hand etc.

(Loss of a pack of wool at the warehouse)

21t (No year).
Mr Rook
        Sir
                I have received your letter respecting the pack of wool your sheet that is left in the warehouse will not do for me I don not want any of that sort of wool my pack that they have got was out of one of the best Stocks in Cumberland and now I cannot buy as good wool as it was for the price that I have chard it to Mr John Robinson
                I am Sir
                      Your most obdt
                          J Dover

(Written to a tanner near Whitehaven when the country was still disturbed after Peterloo)

1819
Decr 31t
Mr Norman
        Sir
                I have recived your letter of the 27th Int in respect to the present prices of Skin wool I cannot judge how it may go I have not been in the skin wool market for sum time we have been mostley working fleece wool of late their is still a large quantity of fleece wool yet unsold in the growers hand it appears that wool is not so much wantd as one has knone it. the general trade in Yorkshire is not good the country is in such a disturbed State that no one can tell how the trade is lickley to be. I shall send you 2 pack

sheets in 3 or 4 weeks for one pack of knitting Wool and one pack of Second wool. etc.

(Character of a young man)

1820 Jany 28th
Mr Wm Spencer
          Sir

                I have received a letter from one William Mackey who sayes that he is beginning business and has lived with you sum years and is in want of goods he say Mr Wm Spencer will satisfy any enquirey you please to make I shall be much obligd to you if you will let me know by return of post if he is a yong man that one may give credit to as I do not know him by name I hope you will excuse me for giving you this trouble.
          I am Sir your most obed
                    Jos Dover

(A new master for the school)

1820 Augt 25t
Mr Jas Hudson
          Sir,

                I have recived your letter of the 23d Int, and I have spoken to Thos Herd and sum more of the neighbours and they all seem quite agreeable to your comeing to the school Thos Herd & I went over to the old master to see to take the hous that he had for a school but as yet he had not made up his mind but be promised that he would let is know in a fewe days and then we shall write you again but in the meen time pleas to write us and say if we must take the house for you and their is tables fixed up which he says that he will sell if him and you can agree for them the rent of the House will be about £2- a year by what we could leern of him
          I remain your welwisher
                    J Dover

Appendix E

(Knows what type of wool to expect)

1820
Decr 4th
Mr Wim Watson
    Sir
        I have received your letter of the 23rd of last month onley this day I am much obliged to you for the offer of Robert Grisdale wool of Patterdale but I think that it will be corse & strong in grane and the price is over high for that sort of wool at present. I should not like to buy at that price I have bought wool the last week which I think is as good as his will be at 9/- and 9/6 per stone their is a good deal of wool yet unsold and now is not so high as it has been
    I am sir
    your obdt
        Joseph Dover

(Ennerdale wool. From a letter to John Turrel, Jan. 18th 1821)

If you can buy the wool in Enerdale at 11/6 or 12/- good and clean you may fill the 9 sheets that is left but we got sum bad washed wool their the last time you had best take a look at it before you buy it if you do not buy wool to full the sheets you can let them by with you in a dry place and turn them over now & then…. etc.

(Charity caps—dyeing & milling)

1821
Apl 19th
Mr Spencer
    Sir
        I have recived your letter of the 4th Int I am sorry to hear that the Charity Caps do not suit you we cannot make so small a quantity to the patron inclosed it being a mixter we cannot mill them with aney other goods but the Same colours to have as maney of that sort as would Mill all together would take from 30 to 36 Dozen and it is a colour that is not much sold aney colour that is died in the caps we can make them for you and I should be glad to serve you
    I am Sir
    your most obedt
        Jos Dover

(Considering removing—Offer of mill—In another letter he is offered a Carding Mill at Coniston)

Heblethwaite Hall
Sepr 7th 1821
Mr Hirst
        Sir
                I have recived your letter of the 4t Int. with the offer of a Mill but Since I returned from Cumberland my land lord came over to ower place and he and I agreed on both for the farm & Mills which I had bid at before if we had not agreead on, I should have had no objections to have given you tryal for your place
        I am Sir
        your most obdt
                Jos Dover

(Knitting wool)

Heblethwaite Hall
Sepr 1821
Mr Norman
        Sir,
                I have this day recived your letter of the 17th Inst I shall take one pack of knitting wool and one pack of second White wool more I hope that you can put the knitting in a 14/0 and second White at 9/- but that matter I must leave to your self it is expected yet that wool will still be lower in price I hope the wool will be good, as some of the last I had, I did not like it. I shall send you two pack Sheets in a little time and you can fill them when it suits you with good wool and I shall remit you for all the wool together or if you be in want please to write me and I will remit you for what I have got
        I am Sir
        your most obedt
                Jos Dover

Appendix E

(Old knitters for complicated work)

1822. Feby 6th
Mr Cooper
        Sir
                I have received your Letter of the 2nd Int Saying that you ar in want of a knitter now the knitters with us is mostly accostomed to one sort of woork it is onley a few of the old Knitters that can manage all sorts of caps and these is not good to meet with at present the knitters is all well employed and they do not like to shift unless they have advantage by it you should have one that is master of knitting all sorts of work and at present I do not know of aney one of that sort that I could recomend to you the wool market in this part is flatt and has been bought of late at 6/6 and sum good lots to 7/–

(Loom borrowed by Mr. Thistlethwaite, probably of Dent. Dawson Bannister was a worsted and stocking yarn manufacturer of Dent.)

Heblethwaite Hall
Mar 21st 1822
Mr Thistlethwaite
        Sir
                I met with Dawson Bannister yesterday, and I was making inquirey after the loom that you borrowed and he pretended he knew nothing about it, and said that I might apply to you and now I have only to say that if the Loom brought back and livered at weaving shop Sedbergh I shall immedeately proceed against and you and him to recover it
        I am Sir your ob Jos Dover

(As above)

Heblethwaite Hall
Apl 10 1822
Mr Jerh Thistlethwaite
                I have received your letter of the 26th of last month I Do not remember that you had any orders from us to let the Loom go to Richd Alderson and that it was to you that it was lent, and you'll be the Man that I must clark for it, and now if you do not deliver up the loom at Sedbergh, I will proceed against you to recover it, and Interest upon it, the time you have had it, as for Bannisters teaser the teaser that you mention I neaver had one of his in my possesion,
        Jos Dover

Old Hand-Knitters of the Dales

(Engaged a spinner)

H Hall
Apl 19th 1822
Mr Anty Atkinson
   Sir
      I have received your letter of the 29th of March I was not then in ymmideat want of a Spinner or I should have ansered you sooner but now I am in want of one that can Spinn on a Billey you did not State whether you were a yong man or a man with a familey or if you have been accostomed to look after the carding ingons if you please to write me by return and lett me know when it would suit you to com if you ar not ingaged I then will write you again befor you com
    I am respectly & ob
      Joseph Dover
      Heblethwaite Hall Sedbergh By Kendal

(The London wholesale trade in coarse woollens)

1822 July 17th
Mr James Spencer
   Sir
      I have received your letter of the 12th Int I think the bissenes that might be done in London in our sort of goods might be of great advantage to both you & I and I should be glad to make a trial of it I know of Some Houses who sell a great many cors wollens to that market that is something like the brown plaidings they are all sold for house cloths and I have known a great maney of the white plaidings sent to the London market but when you get fixt in London you will find what sort of goods you can dispose of as we could make them to suit the market I know of one house that is fully employed in making a sort of Stout goods that is all put up for Coat Collars now if you will have the goodness to Send me a pattern of that Sort of Cloth Such as you put up for that purpose and state the bredth and price I shall be much obliged to you as their is a great maney of them sold in London we make a good maney Caps & Bonnets which I think you would find Sale for if you will please to write me and state upon what terms you will transact Busines for will much oblige
    Sir
      Your most obedt Servt
       Jos Dover

Appendix E

ps if you send a pattrn of cloth please send it by Lofthous Coacht to be left at Kings Armes Sedbergh for Josh Dover Heblethwaite Hall

(A Fanny and Stricle are a blower and grinder used in sharpening)

Heblethwaite Hall
Oct 4th 1822
Mr Thos Musgrove

I received your account and after looking it over I find your charges is most extravagant; I neaver ordered the new fanney that you sent and therefore as it is charged so high I shall return it; and I find the strikle for grinding the cards is charged 5s which out of all reason and the guide pully which is charged 3s 6d. is most unreasonable charge and as we neaver have used it I must return it and many other charges is out of all bounds

Jos Dover

(From John son of Joseph to an Uncle in London—about bad times, prices, local news etc)

Heblethwaite Hall 22nd Nov 1822
Dear Uncle

As opportunity falls out to send a letter by a private hand Mr Robt Wallas I have taken the liberty to write a few lines to you as it is now such a long time since we heard for you Father thinks you have forgot us all the farming trade in this Country is very Bad the most of the farmers is broke up my Landlord has sold up to his Tenants and he likely to keep some of the Farms in his own hand as he cannot get it let and if things go in in the state they are in the farming trade will go to nothing we have lately sold three horses for under £20 and there were good Bluecaster Sheep sold at the sale for 2/4 per head. Do you think you could assist us in the sale of the Charity caps in London if you could it would oblige us at the present time as we have a good stock of them upon hand last week Wards and Bluecaster Sides Estates were sold by private contract for £985. We should have sent you some more moor birds but they scarse can be got for money lately as the carrier from Kirkby Stephen to Kendal was conveying some Moor Birds they were seized and the Man was fined £5 as they had not been lawfully got Father would be glad to hear from you by return my Father & Mother and all Friends join me in love to you hoping you are all well as we are all present

I remain your most affect nephew
J Dover

Old Hand-Knitters of the Dales

(To Henry Dover–? in want of a spinner)

Heblethwaite Hall Decr 16 1822
Dear Brother
                        As opportunity falls out to send a letter by Mr Sanders I have just wrote you a few lines saying I am now in want of a good Billy or a Jack Spinner if there is any about Keswick that wants employment of that sort I could now find work but a Single Man would suit best if you'll please to make inquiry and let me know what you make out I shall write you again by return and let you know when he might come.
                I am Dear Brot
                    your Joseph Dover

(There were several families of Dover in the Keswick district)

H Hall Sepr 8th 1822
Dr Cusin
                      We are now in want of a good Spinner if you will please look out about Keswick for one I understand there is one at the Stain Mill that married one of Aunt Marys Daughter and if he inclines to come I shall find him constant work and a house close by to live in, if not any other likely person that you can meet with he may come immediately. I hope you got well home with all your luggage of stones I would be much oblige to you if would get me a pound of well cured rauns (roes) to fish with and send them with the person coming. I will pay you when I come to Keswick Please to give My respects to my Uncle and Aunt hoping you and Grandmother are all well as we are all at present & I remain
                For Father
                    your affect Cousin
                        Jo Dover

(Daniel Dover is a woollen manufacturer at Keswick)

Heblethwaite Hall Apl 9th 1823
Mr Danle Dover
        Sir
                  I understand that you have had a turn out amongst your weavers I should be much obliged to you if you would inform me what prices you are now giving for Different Sorts of Goods and likewise your prices of spinning of Kersey Weft and Warp, plaiding Weft and Warp, check Weft and Warp and if you should have more orders this season than you can

Appendix E

supply your self & I shall be glad to serve on as low terms as you can get them done at Keswick my respects to Mrs D and all family and by so doing will much oblige

        Sir your most obedt
                Jos Dover

(Under the Poor Law of the time they were allowed assistance from the parish if their wages were insufficient)

Heblethwaite Hall July 5th 1823
Mr John Herd
               I now state to you the Situation George Cowperthwaite family is now in they are eight in family and have only two bed for the whole and very much in want of Clothing he is likely to have an increase of family very shortly and now since you have taken half a peck of meal of him I have been obliged to advance him such nessesarys as his family required or they would actually have taken harm, he now can not do with less than a peck and a half a meal per week and there is now £2 due for Rent, if something be not done to assist him and that the family can live upon I shall not continue him here to hunger and starve

      I am ob
           J. Dover

(A roundabout method of payment)

Heblethwaite Hall Augt 14
1823
Mr Mattw Dobson
       Sir
             I recived your letter with an account which Geo Dixon told me he had settled with you, but as I suppose he has not by your letter I now inclose you a Note value one pound, which will settle your account and leave a Ballance of five shillings due which you will please to pay to Mattw Hunton Miller of Wensleydale who attends your market and he may pay it to Mr John Benson of Sedbergh that attends Hawes Market and you and I must settle these matters when we meet as I have not been at Leyburn for some time. I am Sir

        yours respecty
             Jos Dover

(Coaching)

H Hall
Decr 20th 1823
Mr Young
   Sir
     When I was in Newcastle on the 12th of October last I sent the Waiter up from Mr Richardsons the Three Indian Kings to your coach office to take me an inside passage in the coach and instead of taking an inside passage he paid you 12 shillings for an outside passage, for which he had no order to do nor I did not go you will please to have the goodness to pay the 12 shillings to Mr Robt Wallas of Sedbergh due to him your attention to the above will much oblige
    your obdt
     Jos Dover

(An over-draft)

Heblethwaite Hall
Feby 4th 1824
Messrs John Wakefield & Son
   Gentlemen
     Please to send me by return 26 guineas in note I perhaps may have occasion to over draugh my account for 2 or 3 months if it be agreeable to you.
   Gentlemen
    your most obedt.
     Jos Dover

(Severe Illness)

Heblethwaite Hall
Apl 8th 1824
Dr Brother
     It is now some time since any Letter has between you and me it is my painful duty to inform you the loss I have had in my family, one son and two Daughters all in course of a few Days Robert and Mary were both interd one grave on Monday the 22nd and Dorothy on Tuesday the 30th of last month, of a violent fever which has broke out in this Country it appears the Doctors does not understand the Complaint as I have had every advice that laid in my power.

Appendix E

I and some more of the Family have been afflicked with the same disease for some time but thank God we are in fair way of recovery may health and happiness attend you and your family, hoping you are all well

    I remain
        affect Brother
            J Dover

(From a letter to J. Turrel dated Octr 26th 1824)

Brough Hill fair took place this last week cattle of every description was in great demand and sold at much higher prices good, horses, and stags (colts), sold at very high prices, stags that was sold last year for 6 or 7 pounds would have fetched 15 or 16 pon the demand for Sheep was so great that the dealers went a distance on the road to meet them and was sold at much higher prices than was expected.... my respects to all friends etc.

(As above dated Aug 5th 1825)

I arrived back home on Sunday evening after a severe hot day, which my horse and me stood extremely well!.... I looked at a good clip in Legbethwaite (near Thirlmere) of J Wilkinson's if you should be over at Keswick races you can try to buy it, but not to give more than 12/– etc.

        signed for Jo Dover
            J Dover

(Prices of machinery)

H H Augt 10 1825
Mr John Blyth
    Sir

        When I saw you last at Sedbergh you said you were in want of a jack I have made inquirey, and have found one which Arthur Croxton has to dispose of, the price is 5 pounds it seems to be a jack that has not done a great deal of work it carries forty spindles.... I have also a good Carding engin to dispose of it has 4 large cylinders and does a carding 24 inches long the price is about 32 pounds, if you should be in want, you can take a ride over and look at it

    Yours ob
        Jos Dover
PP The Cylinders are all made of Mahogany–

Old Hand-Knitters of the Dales

(From a letter to J. Turrel dated Oct 28th 1825)

... Give my respects to Mr A Sisson and tell him that present Calving Cows, are very high with us, there was two bought lately by our Neighbours the one was £20 the other was 30 pounds but they were of Shorthorned breed. Sedbergh Fair will be holden to morrow, we are expecting a very dear Fair!

etc Jos Dover

(Shuttles and tazzles)

Mr Robert Kelsall
　　　　　Sir
　　　　　　　　Sometime ago Mr Thos Handley, got me some shuttles of you I am at present in want of a few more you will oblige me by forwarding as under

　　6 fly shuttles a gin long & 2/8 wide
　　3 fly Do 15½ in long
　　4 pair of large pickers
　　¼ pack of strong Tazzels for raising Blankets with

please to send a bill along with them, and I shall pay the money to Mr John Holm of Sedbergh, or to your order

　　　　I am Sir your most obdt
　　　　　　　　Jos Dover

(From two letters to J Turrel dated Jany 13th & Feby 22nd 1826)

... There arose such a sudden revolution amongst Banks that I deemed it more prudent both for you and me, to decline remitting you any money till the storm had partly ceased... at the same time say how the Whitehaven Bank is likely to wind up, as there are a quantity of Notes in this country I hope you and your friends is not likely suffer much by that concern as I am afraid it will not turn our very favorable, fortunately for me I have so far steered clear of bad notes and bills but we find it likely to have a very great effect upon the country, every thing almost is on the decline, and Credit worne out at elbows, wool is an article of considerable reduction, and not much inquired after.

There has been another severe run amongst the Banks in this part of the country caused by the failures of a bank at Lancaster and another at Manchester but they all have stood their ground and have established their Credit on a better footing than ever, etc.

Appendix E

(To the same dated Aug 20th 1826)

Wool is likely to be an article of little value, under half of last years price... we have finished our hay and almost done cutting Corn but very light crops. No demand for cattle and a very bad prospect for trade in general.

(From a letter to Daniel Dover of Keswick from Heblethwaite Hall Sept 20th 1826)

I have bought a quantity of coarse wool, such as is grown in this part, at 5/- to 5/6 the price of the same wool last year was 10/- to 10/6 At present the trade is quite at a stand and as there has been some little buying lately, the others is looking for a little more which is not submitted to us yet, and which way it may turn I am not able to judge. Trade is slowly reviving but prices low I hope your trade will be in a more settled state, that what has been experienced in different parts. I should like to know how brother William makes out in his trade my respects to Mrs D and Family etc.

(From a letter dated Sepr 29th 1826 to Mr Allan Simpson asking his opinion of the wool market)

It is my opinion it will be better to buy in a few months time if the Yorkshire people (West Riding manufacturers) keep away, your information by return will oblige.

**(Description of Kilmarnock Caps.
The most interesting letter in the ledger)**

Heblethwaite Hall
Nov 23rd 1826
Mr Danl Dover

       Dr Sir

                Yours I duly recd you may perhaps think me long in sending them, but as I am not in the habit of making the Kilmarnocks at present I have had some difficulty in procuring them, however I have got you 2 finished and 2 unfinished, which I expect will answer your purpose I have also inclosed you a sample of yarn which is knitt double with 2 knitting sticks 9 pair of needles, and a cap board. The quantity of caps we have in 16lb of Blue red & white clean Yarn is 5Doz 4 that is 4 caps to the pound—We mill from 30 to 36 Doz in one stockful, they are put loose into the stocks, and milled with about 8 pounds of dry fullersearth dissolved in water, when they are about half Milld they are taken out and well stretched out, after they are sufficiently

Milld they are taken out and put upon boards and raised wet with fine Cards, they are dryed on the boards, and after that they are a little raised before they are packed up. The price we pay for knitting is 3/9 to 4/- per stone 5 doz 4 (64), they are sold at about 7/- per Doz. I think unless you have a knitter that has been accustomed to knitting these Caps you will not be able to manage them, should you fail in the atempt I would advise you to have a knitter from this part, any further information you may require, I shall do all in my power to assist you with my best respects to you and Family

     I am your odb
      J Dover

(Export trade probably to West Indies and Colonies—From a letter to Mr John Betham of London dated Sept 18th 1828)

  Dr Sir
    We have forwarded to you by the Canal a Bale of Kilmak Caps in order that you might receive sooner than what you would by sea you will please have the goodness to forward them into the market as soon as possible the season is now on for the exportation of these articles, and probable in a few months there will be not so may sold. We are now rapidly increasing in the Manufacturing of these Goods and shall be able to supply you with any quantity that you may find demand for. etc....

(Twisted Yarn)

Heblethwaite Hall Feby 5th 1830
Messrs I & I Allison
  Gentlm
    Yours of the 3 int we recd this morning but we do not rightly understand whether you require this yarn to be sent twisted or not, if it be the case we are sorry to say that at present we have not convenience for twisting it We could spinn you a few packs of it single same quality as sampl and a little smaler if required at 5/6 per stone and if you could favor us with a few packs af any kind of single yarn we should feel obliged—If it should be convenient for you to make us a remittance between and 25th Inst we should esteem it a favor of you

    Jos Dover & Son

Appendix E

(Knitting. From a letter to Messrs Willm. & John Kynaston Dec 2nd 1830)

We are sorry to understand that those Frocks you recd does not meet with your approbation—we were not aware that you required them to be much tighter knitt than the Spottd Frocks, or otherwise we could soon have remedied that without any inconvenience whatever—In future we shall take care not to have the fine Frocks so slack, and likewise pay more regard to the quality, We have at present on hand and out at Knitters about 120 doz which if you could have taken in we should esteem it as a favour, as at present we have no other opening for such goods—With regard to the stockings we should have been happy to have supplied you with these articles but we are afraid our knitters would not manage them properly as they have not been much accustomed to Knitt such stockings as you have described—If you should be in want of Kilk Caps Bonts or Dutch Hats etc. we shall be able to supply you with those articles at this season of the year on reasonable terms.—etc

(Extension of business; and disturbances connected with Parliamentary Reform)

Heblethwaite Hall Dec 9 1830
Dr Brother

In consequence of speculating rather extensively in wool this last year, and likewise extending our business a good deal—we find that we shall require a supply of cash for a few months to the amt of one or two Hundred Pounds—I beg leave to say that I should esteem it as a favor if you could accomodate me with that sum for that period, and I should allow you Interest for the same—

I should suppose from Dealings I have had with Kynaston's House that there is no reason to be afraid of crediting them to large amount—You probably might be able to give me some information respecting them if you would have the goodness to speak to some of your friends on the subject in such a manner as will not give it any publicity. Their Acct with us for the last few months will exceed a thousand pounds and the acct is gradually increasing as we send them a supply of goods now weekly—

We are now fully employed in our Trade and can scarsely get a sufficient quantity of goods made. I certainly feel much obliged to you for your kindness in sending me the paper and particularly at this present time as the papers now treat on subjects from which I derive much interest—I am glad to find that the commotion you have had in your large City lately is gradually drawing to a close I trust that you will not have experienced any bad effects from it. etc.

Old Hand-Knitters of the Dales

(A man dismissed for ill-treatment of children)

Feby 3 1831

... he not only absented himself from his work without leave but also when he was at work he created nothing but disturbance amongst the other work people by his abusive language and likewise he had without any cause whatever knocked down and abused some of the children in the mill. etc.

(From a letter to Messrs John Dixon & Co Feb 28th 1831)

We can at present supply you either 1000 doz of Kilk Caps which will average in weight about 2 lbs 7 ounces at 5/10 per dozen, and should you require a quantity of the heavier ones to weight 2¾ lbs per dozen we shall be able to supply you with a quantity of these at 6/4 per dozen. etc.

(First business letter to I & R Morley of London)

Heblethwaite Hall May 6th 1831
Messrs I & R Morley

Bot of Jos Dover & Son

lbs									
9½	4 doz	Corse	Spottd	jkts	No 1	@ 15/6	3	2	0
8¼	4 doz	Comm.	Do	Do	No 2	@ 17/-	3	8	0
9¼	4 doz	Do	Do	Do	No 3	@ 18/-	3	12	0
10½	4 doz	fine	Spottd	Do	No 5	@ 23/6	4	14	0
11½	4 doz	Do	Do	Do	No 6	@ 25/6	5	2	0
13	2 doz	fine	Do	Do	No 7	@ 29/-	2	18	0
10¼	1 doz	Comm	White	Do	No 3	@ 20/-	4	0	0
10½	1 doz	fine	Do	Do	No 4	@ 23/6	1	3	6
11½	1 doz	fine	Do	Do	No 5	@25/6	1	5	6
13	1 doz	fine	Do	Do	No 6	@ 29/-	1	9	0
14½	1 doz	fine	Do	Do	No 7	@ 32/-	1	12	0
			1 wrap 5¼ yds					3	6
Cwt	qr	lb					32	9	6
2	3	10 wgt.	4 months and Bill at 2m dis				1	12	6
			By our cart to Kendal ent				30	17	0

Appendix E

Gentlm
According to your obliging order we have sent you as samples of our Froxs, different sorts as described in the annexed invoice, we trust you will find these goods to answer your purpose, and should you be able to favour us with a further order we shall endeavour to serve you with a good article as reasonable as possible.
We are gentlm
yours etc
J Dover & Son.

(About I & R Morley and presents sent—
From a letter to Mr John Betham May 7th 1831)

… I am sorry to say that the package of Hams I only packed of yesterday but I trust you will excuse me when I have mentioned what has been the cause of this dalay. A few days before I entended sending them off Aunt Brunskill told me she intended to send you and miss Betham each a pot of trout, and if I could delay sending them for a few days they would be ready to go along with the Hams—But however as fish is very scarse this season they were not ready so soon as expected, Yesterday I addressed to you Water Lane carrg paid 2 pots of Fish and a small Bundle of letters along with some oat Bread which I hope you will receive safe. We sent you also yesterday a Bale ofFroxs as sample to Messrs I & R Morley Wood Street, I should feel obliged to you if you would have the goodness to wait upon them after you have got your parcel, to know if the Frox suit and to solicit a further order etc

(Complaints to Dyer)

He Hall Nov 2nd 1831
Mr John Blyth
Sir
We have only lately commenced to mill and finish the Caps made from the yarn you dyed us—and after milling them they are certainly such a colour as never was produced by any person who knows anything about dyeing it is doubtful whether we can sell at any price if we can dispose of them it can only be done by making a great sacrifice in the price—if we were to give you nothing for dyeing this (as it certainly does not deserve anything) it would not cover the loss we shall sustain by it—if you wish to see the colour we can send you a cap to convince you of the facts stated
yours etc J Dover & Son

Old Hand-Knitters of the Dales

**(The best knitters made the fine frocks—
From a letter to Messrs Wm & John Kynaston Aug 7th 1832)**

We have this day forwarded you by way of Stockton 4 Bales of Goods.... Should you be in want of any of the lower spottd Froxs, we should be glad to supply your orders on the same terms as the last, we have about 2 or 3 hundred don of them on hand We have also about 200 doz Logd Kilk Caps on hand, if you could favor us with an order for the whole we shall put them in @ 5/- per Dozen our prices for Indigo Blue Kilk Caps is now 5/9 per Dozen.... We are now going on with your order for fine spottd and White Frocks, but as you mentioned you were in no particular want of them, we only employ a few of our best knitters with them... etc.

(Knitters)

July 16th 1835
Messrs Wm & J Kynaston
        Gentlm
                Ever since we recd your letter for the Comn Spottd Frox we have done all that laid in our power in order to supply you with the quantity you required; but we find it impossible to get them except in small quantities, we expect to be able to forward you a small Bale in a few days— The reason why Frocks are so difficult to get made at this present time is in consequence of the great demand there has been for other sorts of goods, so that we cannot get them to Knitt Frocks when they can get lighter work although we have advanced the price of Knitting full 30 per ct. this last 2 months our stocks of Frocks at present are about

50 doz	White	No 5	11 lbs	@	27/-
50 doz	do	6	12 lbs	@	29/-
50 doz	do	7	13 lbs	@	31/-
100 doz	Spottd	5	11 lbs	@	24/-
40 doz	do	6	12 lbs	@	26/-
100 doz	do	7	12½ lbs	@	28/-

If these Frocks will answer your purpose we shall be happy to forward them providing we are favored with an early reply
            etc. Jos Dover & Son

the original glove tops

Appendix F
NEW TO THIS EDITION

George Walton Gloves

"In Deep-dale (near Dent) the farmers principally employ themselves at home in sorting and carding wool for knitting...."
—*The Old Hand-Knitters of the Dales,* Hartley and Ingilby. p. 91

A T the Wordsworth Trust's Museum in Grasmere, Cumbria, two beautifully intricate, hand-knit gloves rest quietly in a display case. The museum has no provenance for this unique pair of fringed gloves; but they are labelled in the display "George Walton, Deepdale, 1846" and have "G. Walton, 1846" knitted into the cuffs. This makes them the oldest extant, dated Dales gloves.

These beautiful specimens therefore have their own story to tell about knitting in the Dales—a story that we will attempt to piece together here. You can then participate yourself in knitting history by working the reproduction pattern on page 151. Thanks are due to Jeff Cowton, MBE, curator, and also to staff at the Wordsworth Trust Museum, who took these gloves out of the display case for us to document, on two visits made in 2012.

∽

The original gloves are worked in natural brown and cream, 2-ply handspun wool, knitted at a gauge of 13 stitches × 18 rounds per inch. Although the gloves are knitted from plied yarn, the 1.5 cm fringe is made from looped singles. The underside, not usually visible when the gloves are on display, is covered all over in a midge and fly pattern. Another thing that became apparent when the gloves were taken from the display case was the intriguing lack of an entire second finger on the right hand glove. The live stitches are held on some yarn. Whether this is a never-completed repair late in the glove's life, or whether Mr Walton needed to give his finger more air—we'll never know!

Old Hand-Knitters of the Dales

Earlier gloves, like earlier stockings, are less likely to have a ribbed cast on. Instead, a short fringe is worked into the cast-on round. This technique of knitting in "ends" or "thrums" was common from the seventeenth century onward in knitted items such as sailors' caps, high-status silk jackets, and New England mittens. The technique was often used for added warmth; here it was used for decoration. The gloves' gauntlet shape and construction are also suggestive of an earlier period.

In Search of George Walton

The Wordsworth Trust had no further information about the G. Walton gloves, or any provenance other than a card that read "G. Walton Deepdale, 1846." Worse still, in *The Old Hand-Knitters of the Dales*, Hartley and Ingilby had interpreted the *G* of his name erroneously as a *C*. Looking at the fragile original, and eyeballing it in person, I was certain the initial read *G*, not *C*. I decided "George" was the most likely forename for our target—having seen thousands of northern English parish record entries. In Georgian times, you can almost guarantee to find every male in a family if you have the surname, by searching for a narrow field of forenames: John, George, Richard, Robert, Henry, James, Joseph, etc. George was the universal boys'-name-beginning-with-a-G, largely due to the fashion for naming sons after royalty. George was the name of both the king and the man who was to become Prince Regent.

I also searched for "Georgina," as some extant gloves are known to have belonged to women, and I knew I would have to eliminate that as a possibility. I had no luck. From slightly later dates, I could find Georginas and Georgianas in London, Birmingham, Somerset, and other far-flung locations, but none in the target area. I decided to narrow my search down to Georges rather than Georginas.

Dales gloves were often knitted as small commissions and so were frequently personalised. One child's glove, housed at the Dales Countryside Museum in Hawes, simply has the name "Mary" on the cuff. Other gloves have initials. Some have names and dates. Less personalised gloves were also knitted in the thousands and sold at market in Kendal, Kirkby Stephen, and further afield. Whoever "G Walton" was, he had had the gloves knitted specially for him, perhaps by a friend or a neighbour—or maybe he had ordered them at a local market and picked them up later—or perhaps a loved one or friend bought them for him as a present.

Appendix F

And here our problems began. There were several possible George Waltons. And several possible Deepdales—in Yorkshire, Lancashire and Cumbria. I was leaning toward assuming this was the Deepdale in Yorkshire, but in *The Old Hand-Knitters of the Dales*, Hartley and Ingilby documented the gloves as being from Deepdale in Cumberland (the older name for the county now called Cumbria).

I decided I could narrow down my search, if I gave some thought to just exactly who might own such gloves and why they ended up in the Wordsworth Trust's Museum at Grasmere, in Cumbria. Knowing they were Dales gloves, I decided to hone in on Yorkshire—or Cumbria, the county where the gloves ended up.

I knew from reading account books from the early nineteenth century that woolly gloves were most likely to be purchased for the elderly or ill. So I decided that "my" George Walton was more likely to have been middle-aged or older by 1846, the date on the welts.

We have further contextual clues. There are only half a dozen or so surviving pairs of Dales gloves out of the tens or hundreds of thousands knitted in the nineteenth century. Of these extant gloves, several appear to have been knitted by the same woman: Mary Allen.[1] Mary died in 1924, and is not the knitter of the 1846 gloves. But her location in Dent gives us the clue as to where the heartland of the Dales gloves knitters lay. The area around Dentdale, including Dent itself and Sedburgh, seems to have been the fulcrum of the entire Dales glove-knitting industry. Sedburgh—in the nineteenth century often called Sedbusk—was in the heart of Deepdale. Gloves from there were sold at Kirkby Stephen and other markets.

All the Wordsworth Trust could tell me was that the gloves were "from Deepdale." There is a Deepdale not too far from Grasmere itself. I had to keep an open mind, initially, as to whether the gloves were Yorkshire-knitted, or Cumbrian. Given that the vast majority of extant Dales gloves were from Yorkshire, not neighbouring Cumbria or Westmorland (which had the same knitting tradition), this suggested possible Yorkshire origins—until I recalled

---

1   A diamond-patterned pair of gloves in the Wordsworth Trust's collection correspond to previously "lost" Dales gloves that have turned up in the collection of the Knitting and Crochet Guild, also thought to be knitted in Dent by Mary Allen.

that Hartley and Ingilby had documented them as being Cumbrian when they visited in 1948 or 1949.

Confusingly, the Deepdale in Cumbria is part of the Yorkshire Dales National Park and sits by one of the Dales' peaks, Whernside. It is the highest point in North Yorkshire, and its summit is on the county border with Cumbria. This meant that if he lived in Deepdale, "my" George might have come from either Yorkshire or Cumbria, since either way he was right on the county borders. Whernside was just a few miles from Dent, the epicentre of Dales glove knitting. The vicinity of Whernside therefore became my target. If I could find a George Walton within a reasonable radius, I had a hot prospect. This also put me close to the county border for Westmorland where many Dales knitters worked.

Woollen gloves were not inexpensive items for working people. The account books of The Retreat, an asylum in York, show that in the summer of 1809 one Benjamin Boynes bought "A Pr of woollen Gloves 1 shilling and 3d" (about 6p in "new money"). If it seems odd that Benjamin purchased woolly gloves in the height of summer, that is probably explained by the next entry in his accounts: "9d Shroud ... Coffin 6 shillings and 3d; Gravemaking 2/6."

For much of the early nineteenth century, a pair of worsted hand-knit stockings would have sold for around two shillings. Most of the cost would have been accounted for by the cost of raw materials, labour being cheaper than wool. G. Walton was thus unlikely to have been either very wealthy or very poor. The gloves with a personalised name knitted into them must have cost slightly more than plain gloves, or gloves with no customisation.

So, to the censuses. In the UK, the first-ever national census was held in 1841. We knew our George was buying gloves—or having them knitted for him by family members—in 1846. I say "family members," as the two gloves are not identical. Even within a single round, the forms of decreases and increases vary. Contemporary accounts mention children each knitting a stocking or glove, or parents knitting the body of the glove and a child the fingers. Looking at the Walton gloves, I felt fairly sure that they were not knitted by a single person and that at some later point in their lives they were heavily repaired by another hand entirely. Parts showed signs of being re-knit in a very similar wool but different tension. And there was that missing finger.

All I had to go on was a G. Walton: most likely George Walton, possibly born in the late eighteenth century, and living somewhere near or in one of the

Appendix F

Deepdales—or living on a feasible trade route to the markets where Deepdale gloves would be sold.

And of course, he may have been somewhere else entirely on census night, or may have lived somewhere else and gone years later to Deepdale. We have no record but the gloves, which were likely to have been donated to the museum at some point in the twentieth century, as earlier than that a holey pair of woollen handspun gloves would have been seen as items of little value.

Yorkshire, Westmorland, and Cumberland were known for their statesmen—small yeoman farmers, holding on to their last few acres of inherited land. Often the statesmen's farmsteads became the knitting schools that flourished in the eighteenth century. These schools spun and knitted their own wool to make gloves and stockings. Dorothy Wordsworth wrote of their neighbour, the statesman Thomas Ashburner, being forced to sell his land. In a desperate bid to keep afloat financially, the Ashburners rose at dawn to card and spin:

> Sent Peggy Ashburner some goose. She sent me some honey—with a thousand thanks.... I went in to set her right about this & sate a while with her. She talked about Thomas's having sold his land ... then she told me with what pains and industry they had made up their taxes & interest &c &c—how they all got up at 5 o clock in the morning to spin & Thomas carded, & that they had paid off a hundred pound of the interest.
> —*Dorothy Wordsworth's 'Grasmere Journal'*, 24th November, 1801, p.41.

My own ancestors, the Stephensons and the Bellas family of Westmorland, were statesmen in neighbouring Ravenstonedale, where they raised fell ponies, kept sheep, spun wool; the small-time farmers were also lead miners on the side. Lead mining was often an extra money-spinner for farmers: lucrative, but very dangerous. It was common for the lead miners not to live much beyond middle age, and they would certainly have suffered from various occupational illnesses if they made it to middle age. It is likely that the George Walton gloves were knitted by the daughters of such a statesman and that George himself may have come from that community.

Now, if my target was alive in 1846, and an adult, he was guaranteed to feature on the 1841 Census. Still, this leaves us with some problems, as that first census had its full complement of glitches. In 1841, the enumerators did not ask for birthplace; they only ticked *Yes* or *No* for whether you were born in the county where you lived on census night.

Also, the 1841 census is notorious for rounding up or down ages randomly by five years or more. So not only might the target's age be inaccurately reported, but there would be no definite birthplace—just whether they were born in Yorkshire (or Cumbria) or not. The census takers did not note marital status or relationships of different people within a household.

By 1851, these issues had been rectified: people had to give their birthplace, and ages were more precise. So when relying on the 1841 Census, you always hope your target will have lived at least until 1851, so that you can clarify things a bit. I knew my George Walton was likely to be middle-aged, so although he was guaranteed to be around in 1841, all bets were off for 1851 or 1861.

Surprisingly, I found only three likely, middle-aged George Waltons in Yorkshire, Westmorland, or Cumbria, for 1841. The first was a man of 60 and a farmer in Middleton, in Ryedale, Yorkshire. He was unlikely to be my man, because Ryedale is nearly 85 miles away.

My second George was a 60-year-old labourer in Brampton, Cumberland, and had been born in Scotland. Brampton was an unpromising 65 miles from the Whernside Deepdale.

And so to my final George. This one was a 50-year-old lead miner in Brough, Westmorland, but not born in the county. As this placed us close to three counties' borders, the likelihood was that he had been born in either Yorkshire or Cumberland. I knew from my own family history research that lead miners were often also from farming families. As Hartley and Ingilby wrote: "miners and their families all knitted.... The thrifty ones often gathered fallen wool, and carded, spun, and knitted it in their own homes" (41).

More clues about our prospective George Walton come from historian William Rollinson, who discussed Westmorland lead mining in his *Life and Tradition in the Lake District*:

> Working conditions in Lakeland mines were harsh and dangerous; in the days before gunpowder, "levels" were cut by hand using picks, hammers ... Although the wages paid to miners were somewhat higher than those of agricultural workers, the arduous conditions and heavy manual work endured by these men brought premature old age and sometimes appalling injuries for which the extra financial reward was no compensation.
>
> *William Rollinson,* Life and Tradition in the Lake District *(Clapham, Lancaster: Dalesman Books, 1981), pp. 164–5*

Appendix F

Further hinting at the long connection between wool and lead in the lives of some Dalesfolk comes from my farming/lead-mining ancestor, Joseph Bellas, who died in 1761 leaving his widow, Ann, "a spinner," living with her son in Long Marton.

Brough had once been part of Kirkby Stephen parish, and this got my attention, as I knew Kirkby Stephen had been a thriving market for hand-knitted goods. Brough was 27 miles away from Dent, but directly on the road to Kirkby Stephen and Dent, in Deepdale. In the eighteenth century Kirkby Stephen had been famous for its stocking trade. In 1754, the following description of the Kirkby Stephen market appeared in the *Gentleman's Magazine*:

> The market is on Monday ... it generally begins around six, and is over about eight in the morning. Tho' the situation of Kirkby Stephen is under bleak and barren mountains, yet the communication with several of their own dales, and with Yorkshire, along the river heads, affords a pretty considerable market, an advantage which Brough near Stainmore has now lost for want of such a connection.
>
> *Quoted in* The Old Hand-Knitters of the Dales, *p. 81*

George lived in Brough, which had once had its own market for woollen goods. He or a relative or friend could easily have bought the gloves on Kirkby Stephen's market.

This being the incomplete 1841 Census, there was no indication of whether George was married or unmarried, but he was living with other lead miners, none of whom shared his surname.

I was unable to find the Brough lead-mining George on the 1851 or any subsequent census. I was also unable to locate a birth record dating from around 1785–1795 for George. I was disadvantaged by the lack of definite birthplace on the 1841 Census, as well as the probable calibration of his age to round figures. Had he been a *Yes* for "birthplace = Westmorland," that would have given me something to go on. Most of the George Walton births that are currently on the parish records on Ancestry.com, are for other George Waltons, people we can tie in to contemporaries who are not our man in Brough. Or they are men in the distant west or South Yorkshire.

Nor could I find the lead miners and lead miner's wife that this George lived with, in either the 1841 or 1851 Census records.

Old Hand-Knitters of the Dales

Finally, I could find no likely marriage records for our man in the decades preceding or after 1841. That is not to say he wasn't married at some point—just that I could find no record of it. In England, marriage certification started in 1837, and it is likely George was married much earlier than this, if he was widowed by 1841. Prior to 1837, you have to look to parish records for details of births, marriages, and burials, and few parish records from the Dales are digitised on Ancestry.com. Hopefully, as more records come online, we may well find our George. In the same vein, George's death is not findable on Free BMD, the go-to site for finding a death registration indexed post 1837. That is not to say he wasn't registered, just that Free BMD's coverage is patchy. Frustratingly, I managed to find deaths in the 1840s and '50s that I could tie in to the other Georges—just not our George.

Still, he left us a legacy: the finest, most complex, and earliest extant dated pair of Dales gloves. In *A History of Hand-Knitting* (p.107), Richard Rutt discussed Lord Howick's gloves, dated 1833 in Leicester Museum; but these do not appear to be Dales gloves or even remotely in the Dales tradition.

Marie and Joan described a pair of gloves they saw, which, like Miss Banks' fringed gloves that Marie illustrated, may be no longer extant. "The pair from Wensleydale which belongs to Miss M. Fawcett of Hardraw is the most elaborate," write Hartley and Ingilby. "The name on the wrist-band is 'Mary Moor's' and the date is 1841" (*Old Hand-Knitters of the Dales*, p. 27).

So we can safely say that the G Walton gloves are the oldest extant, dated pair of Dales gloves—and the only extant fringed pair that are currently known.

Appendix F

original gloves—palm side

Appendix F

GEORGE WALTON GLOVES

Reverse engineered by "Corvid," Tom van Deijnen, and Penelope Lister Hemingway

This pattern allows you to create your own modern version of the historic George Walton gloves. In the original pair, there do appear to be minor inconsistencies between the left and right glove. The reconstructed pattern that we've provided here is taken from the left glove—and reversed for the right, as a result!

If you want to substitute your own name for G Walton's, you have a round of 80 stitches to play with, and the capital letters are charmingly inconsistent; his *G* and his *W* are slightly offset, with the latter a round lower and both 7 rounds tall. The lowercase letters vary in height from 4 to 7 rounds tall. Initial, surname, and date are separated by a single dot that lies 2 or 3 stitches from the neighbouring letters. The lettering's lack of uniformity adds to its charm.

Materials

Jamieson & Smith Shetland Heritage (100% pure Shetland wool; 120 yds/110m per 25g ball)
- [MC:] Flugga White, 2 balls
- [CC:] Peat, 2 balls

US#000/1.5 mm needles, configured for circular knitting
Yarn needle

Gauge

13 sts × 18 rnds = 1 inch square in colorwork pattern

Pattern Notes

For ease of reference in the pattern below, MC is typically referred to as the Lt yarn or just Lt, while CC is called Dk yarn or Dk.

The first two rows in this pattern are knitted flat, then the gloves are joined in the round. If you want an easier alternative for making your loops, refer to the Fringe—Easy Alternative diagram on the following page. But the following method will give you a closer reproduction of the original glove.

Old Hand-Knitters of the Dales

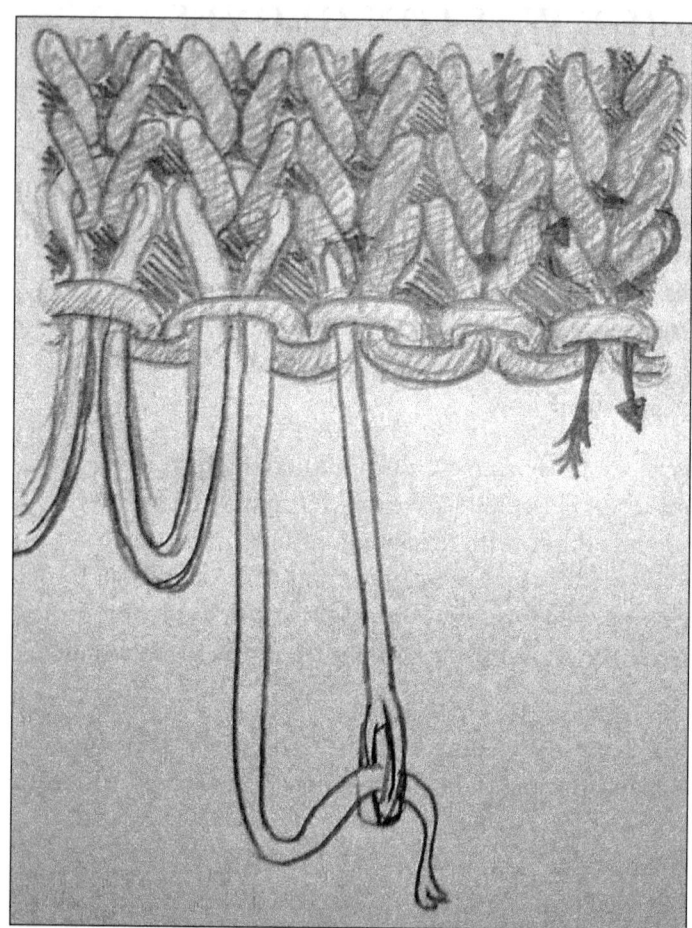

FRINGE—EASY
ALTERNATIVE

Pattern

Row 1: Using Dk yarn and long-tail cast on, CO 78 sts and turn.

Row 2:

- Step 1: Knit 1 st with Dk and Lt held together.
- Step 2: Insert right needle into st on left needle, pick up Lt and wrap it around left index finger and right needle. Drop Lt, and keep loop in place, then pick up Dk and also wrap it around left index finger and right needle. Make sure that when both yarns are on needle, the Dk yarn doesn't cross over the Lt yarn.
- Step 3: Knit both sts and carefully take left index finger out of loops—4 sts on needle, with Dk closest to needle tip.

Appendix F

- Step 4: Repeat Steps 3 & 4 to last st.
- Step 5: For last st, hold Dk and Lt together and knit 1 normal st (no loops formed) and turn.
- Step 6: Drop Lt and carefully knit with Dk to end, treating each doubled-up st as one.
- Step 7: Straighten up the loops, carefully pulling on them whilst holding the cast-on row, to make the doubled sts smaller and the loops larger.

Tips: It is possible to wrap with both yarns held together, as long as you make sure that the Dk loop is always closest to the tip of the needle. When having finished Step 6, the sts should alternate as 1 Dk, 1 Lt. For Step 7, it helps to keep the sts as close to the needle tips as possible, as this will put the least amount of stress on the loops, making the straightening up easier.

The above completes Rows 1 & 2 of the Nameband Chart. Join in the round and commence with Rnd 3 in the Nameband Chart. Refer to Alphabet Chart to use your own name or initials on the welt section.

Rnd 23: Left hand: work Left Palm Chart, Left Thumb Chart, Left Front Chart. Right hand: work Right Front Chart, Right Thumb Chart, Right Palm Chart.

Continue working charts as set, working the M1's where placed (these form the thumb gusset), until you have completed Rnd 51 and have 31 thumb sts on your needles. Slip these sts onto waste yarn, and CO 21 sts in that space.

Continue working the Palm and Front Charts as set. You will complete the Thumb Chart after the fingers have been completed.

Continue to follow charts as set until you have completed Rnd 80. As you can see from the Palm and Front charts, each finger placement has been color coded. Follow each Finger Chart, completing one before moving onto the next, starting with the pinkie and working across the hand until the index finger is completed.

After completing the last round of each finger, break the yarns and thread through the last rnd of sts, pull tightly, and weave in ends. Complete thumbs in same manner.

Old Hand-Knitters of the Dales

Key for all charts

- ☐ MC
- ■ CC
- M make 1
- ∕ k2tog
- ∕ k3tog
- ▨ no stitch
- ■ Stitch allocation for index finger
- ■ Stitch allocation for middle finger
- ■ Stitch allocation for ring finger
- ■ Stitch allocation for pinkie finger

Nameband Chart

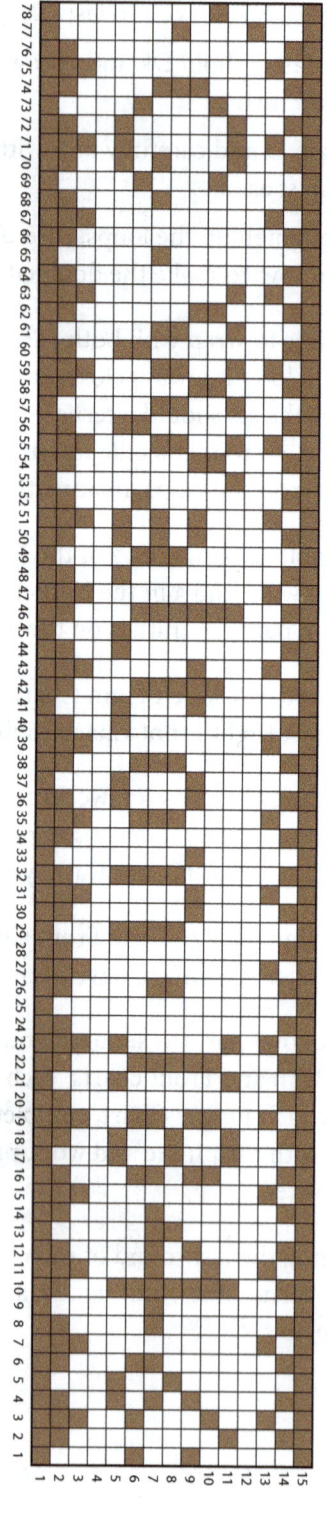

Appendix F

Alphabet Chart

Old Hand-Knitters of the Dales

Left Palm Chart

Appendix F

Left Thumb Chart

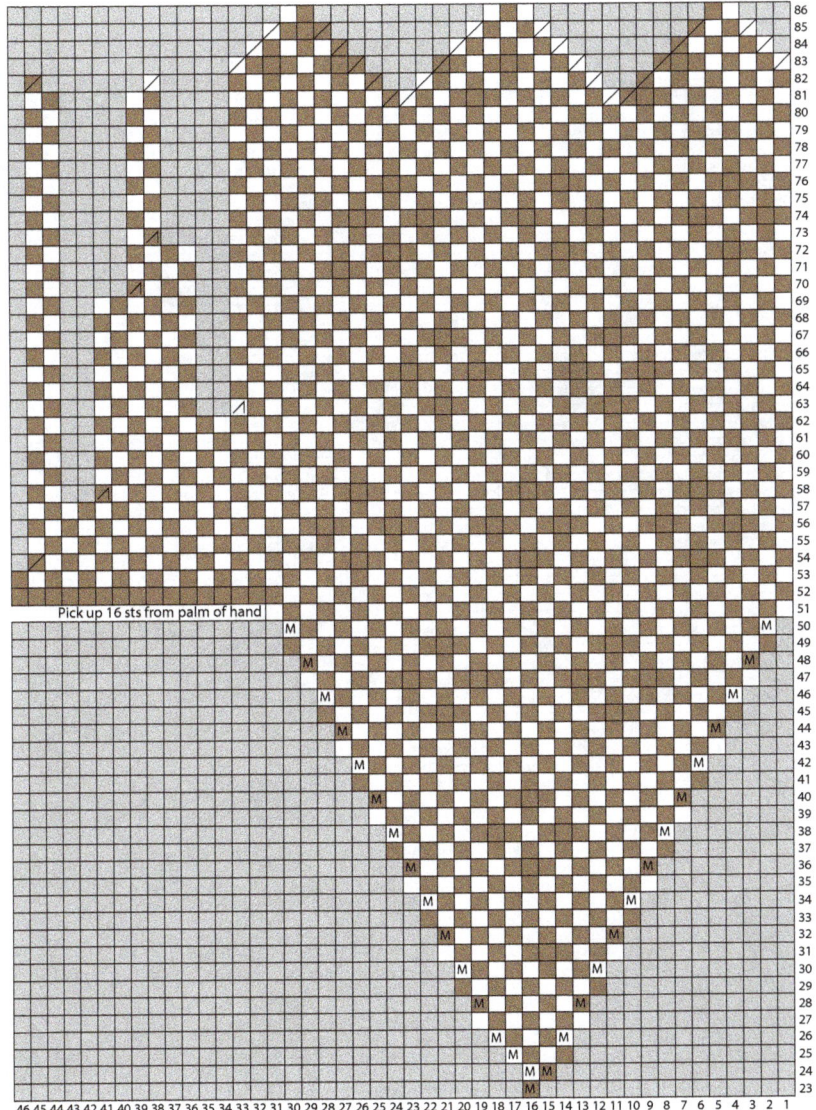

Old Hand-Knitters of the Dales

Left Front Chart

Appendix F

Right Front Chart

Old Hand-Knitters of the Dales
Right Thumb Chart

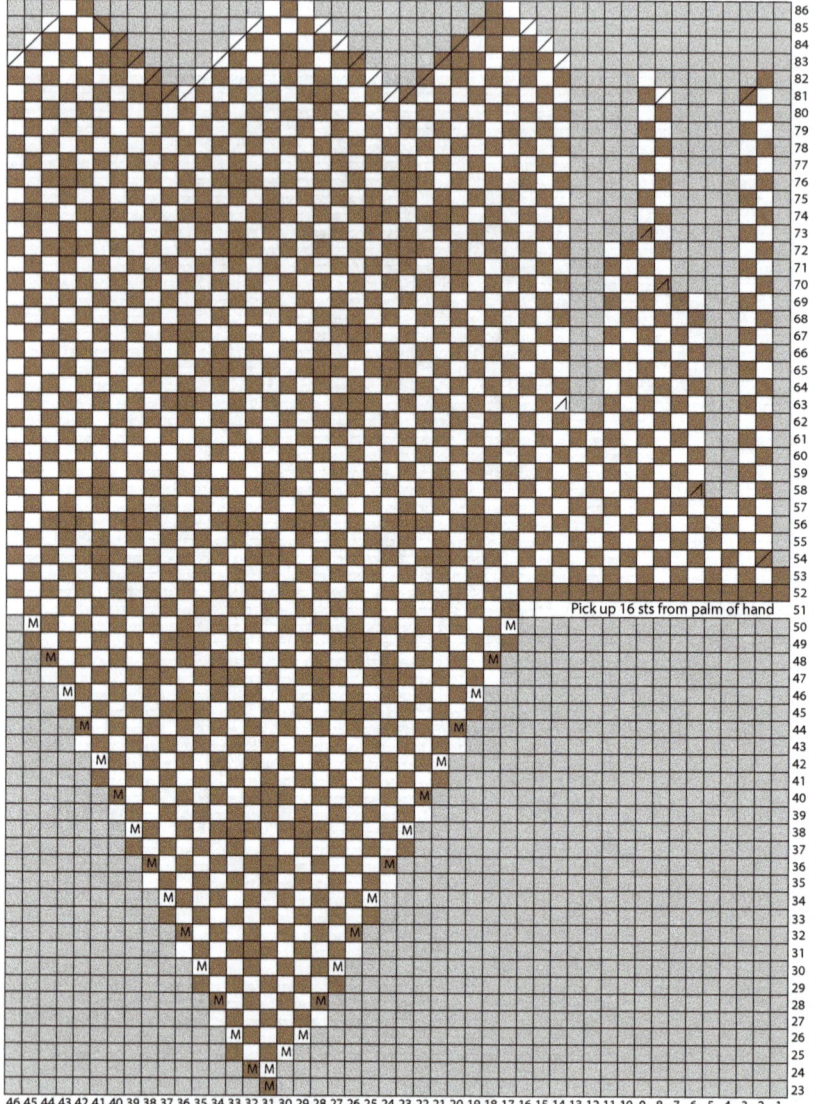

Appendix F

Right Palm Chart

Old Hand-Knitters of the Dales

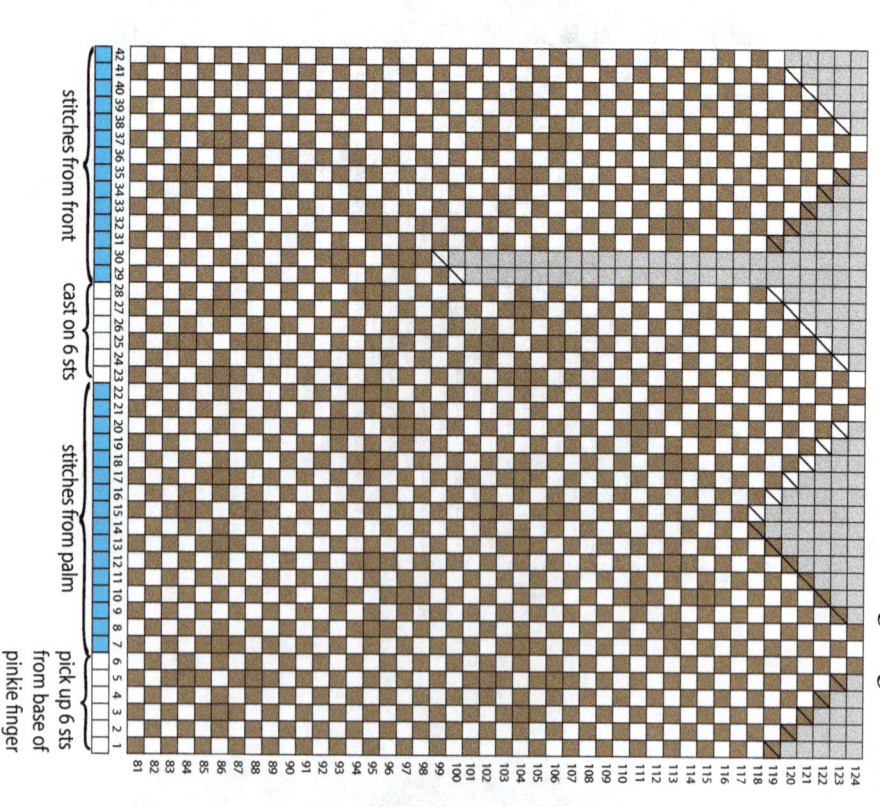

Appendix F

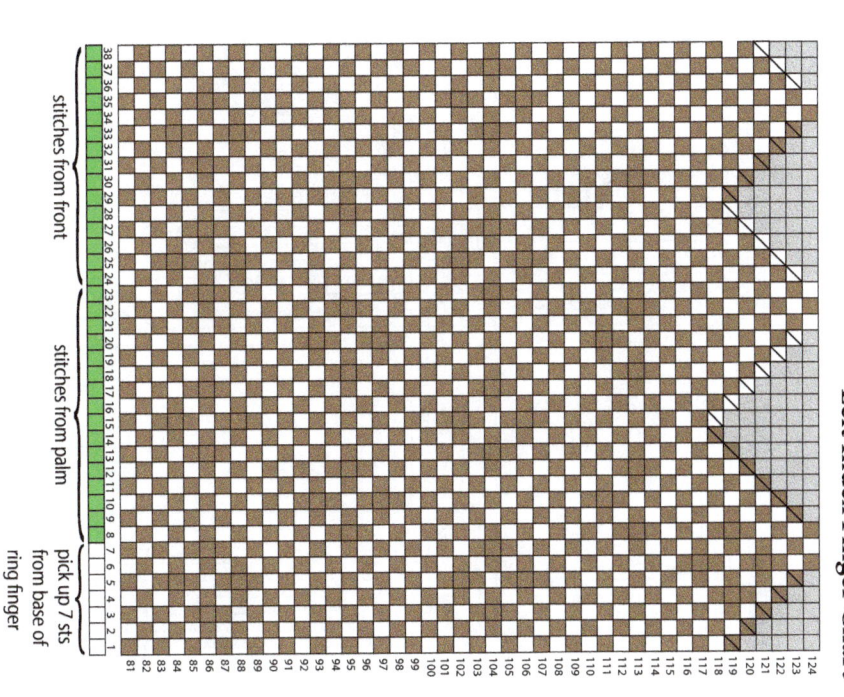

Left Middle Finger Chart

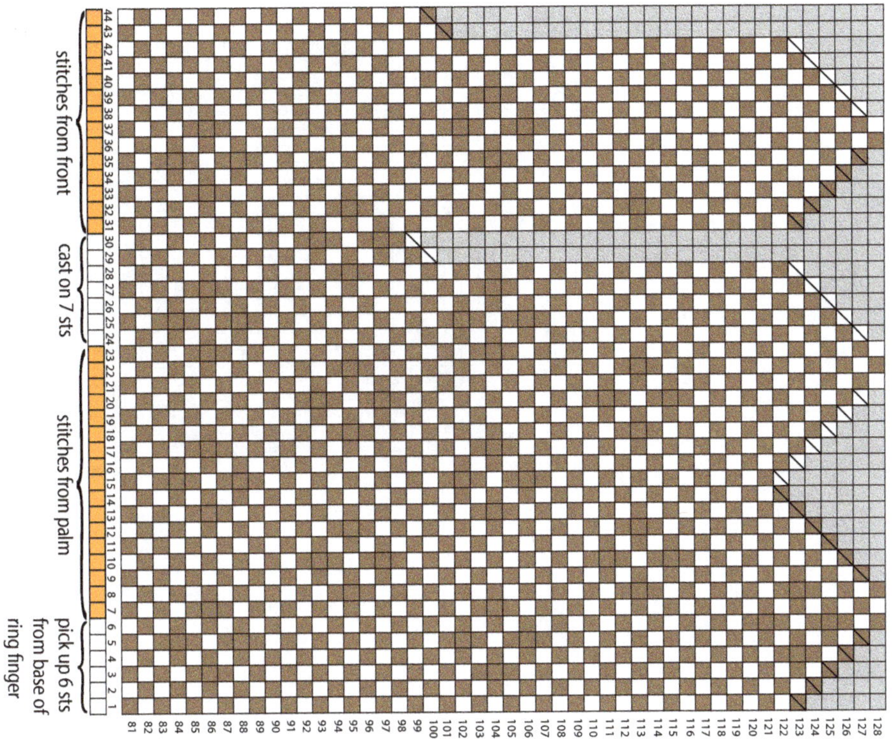

Left Index Finger Chart

Old Hand-Knitters of the Dales

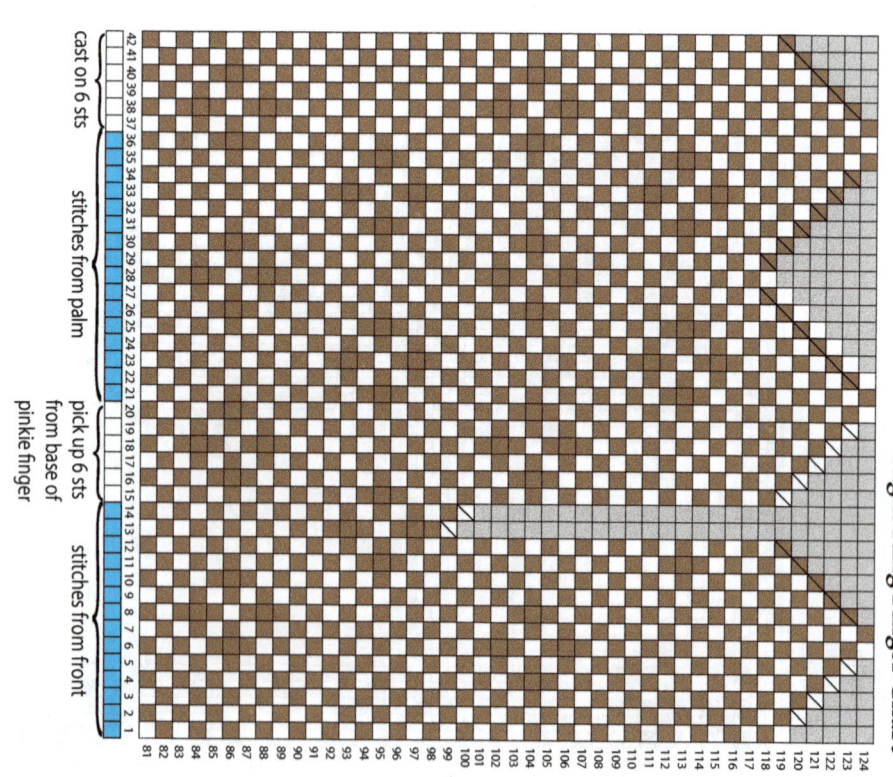

Appendix F

Right Middle Finger Chart

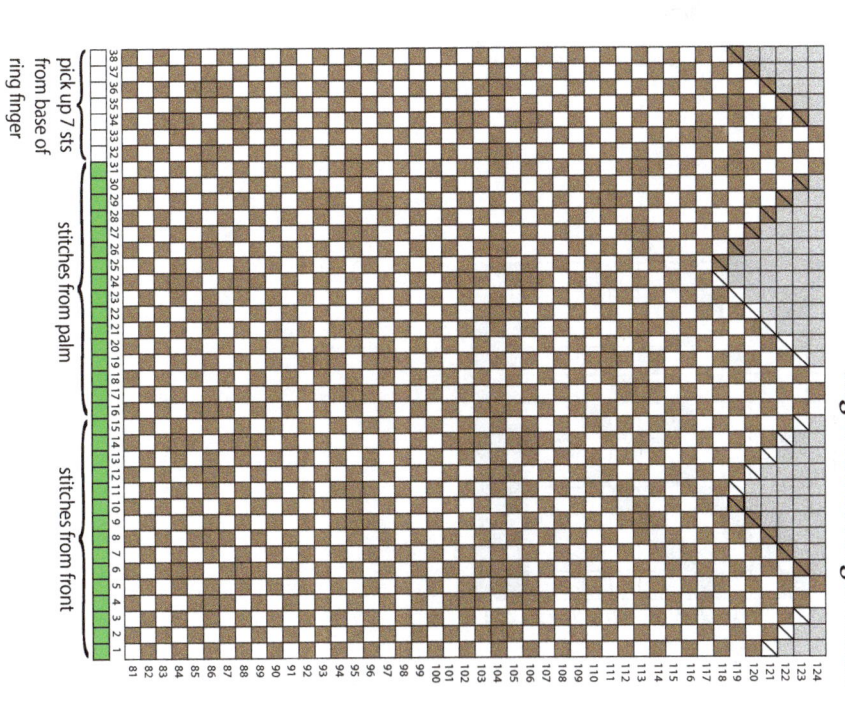

Right Index Finger Chart

Old Hand-Knitters of the Dales

Substitute Stitch Patterns

For use with the blank charts that begin on page 167.

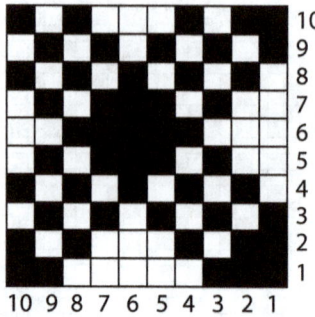

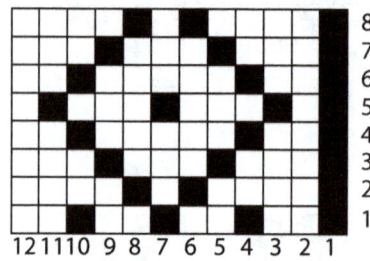

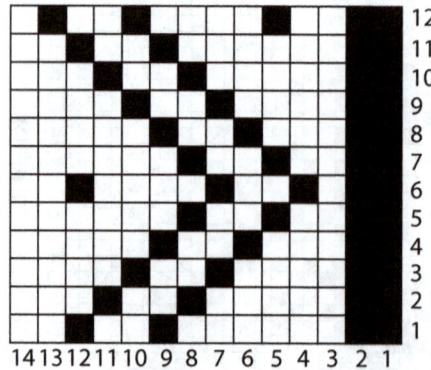

Appendix F

Blank Left Palm Chart

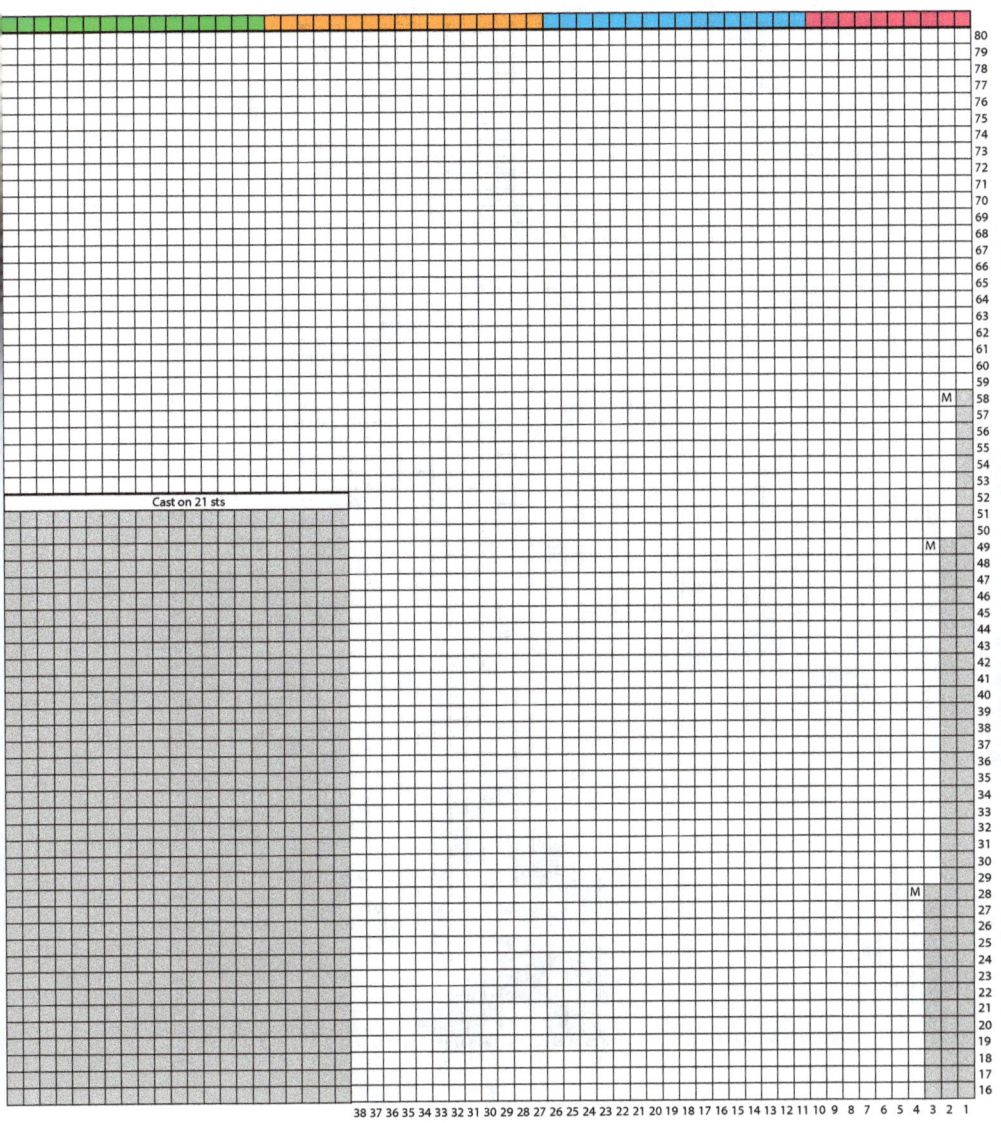

The basic directions for the George Walton Gloves can be used as a template for the other gloves illustrated on page 28 as follows:
1. Choose your desired substitute stitch pattern (page 166)—or create your own substitute stitch patterns.
2. Transpose the pattern onto the blank charts that begin on this page.
3. Otherwise follow directions for the George Walton Gloves (page 151).

Old Hand-Knitters of the Dales
Blank Left Thumb Chart

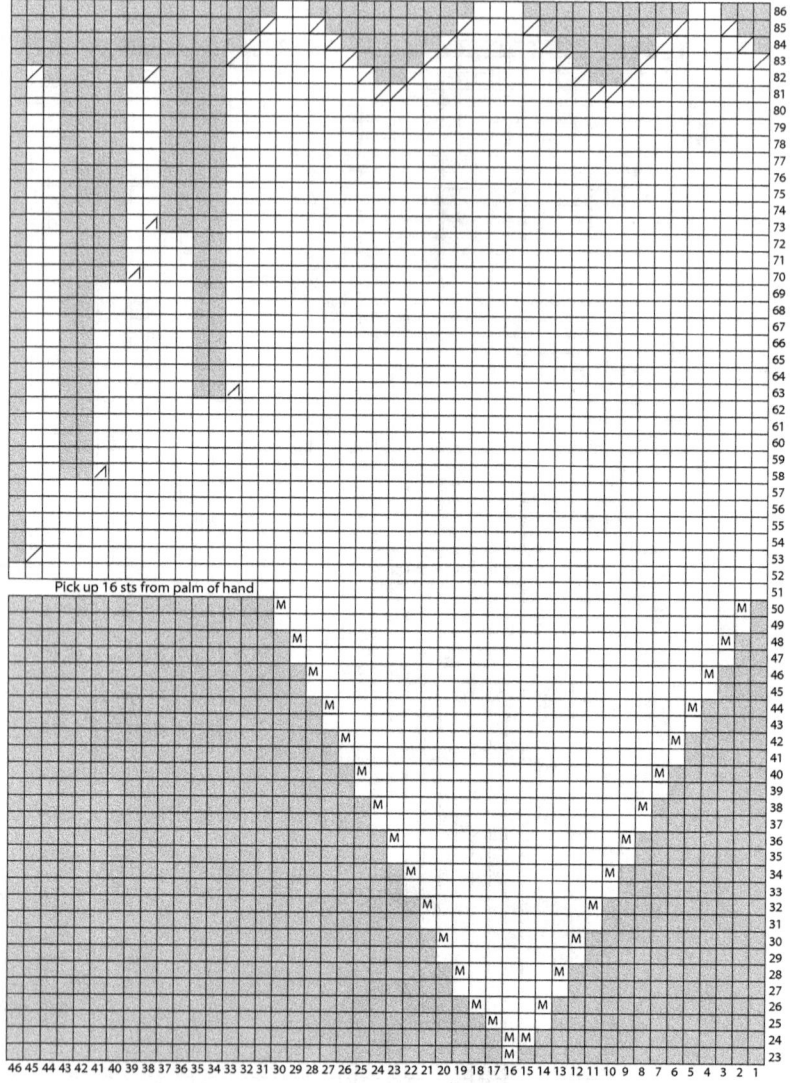

Appendix F
Blank Left Front Chart

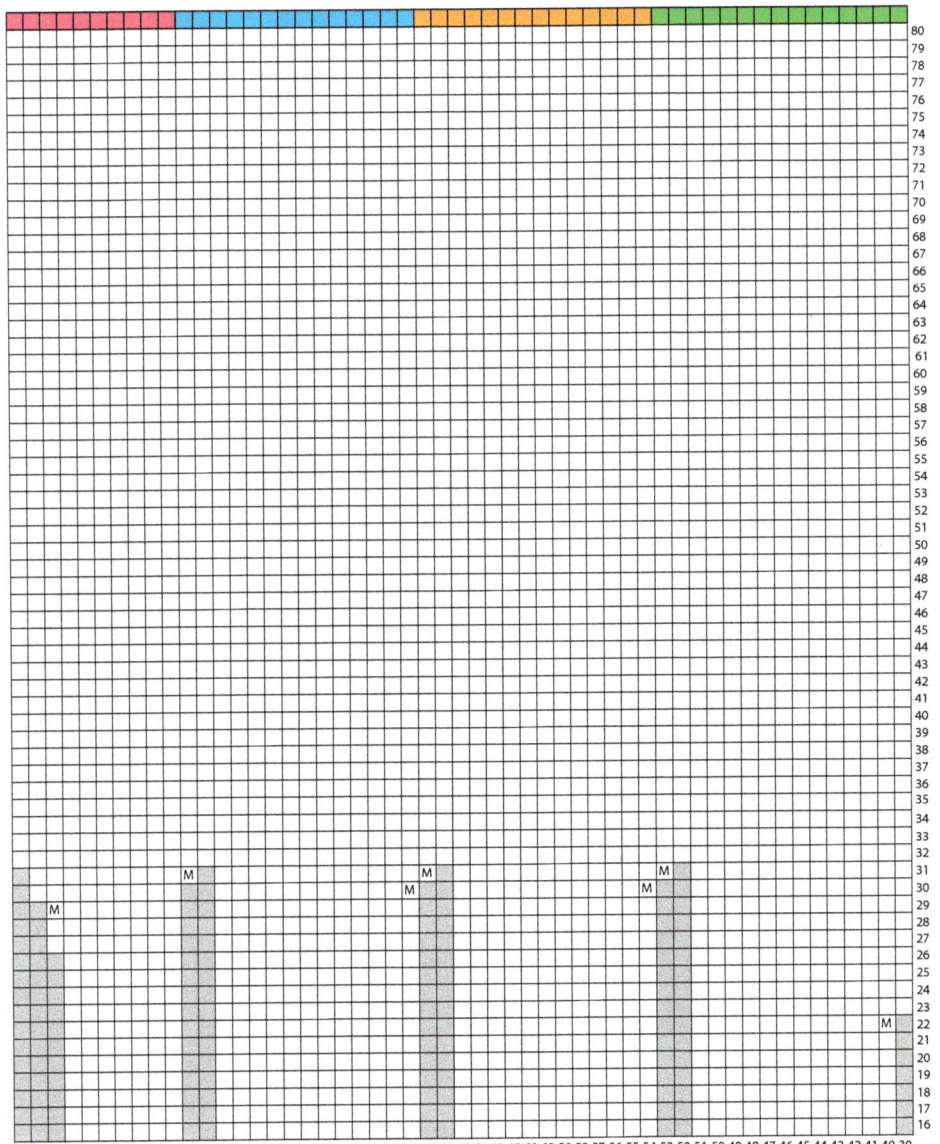

Old Hand-Knitters of the Dales
Blank Right Front Chart

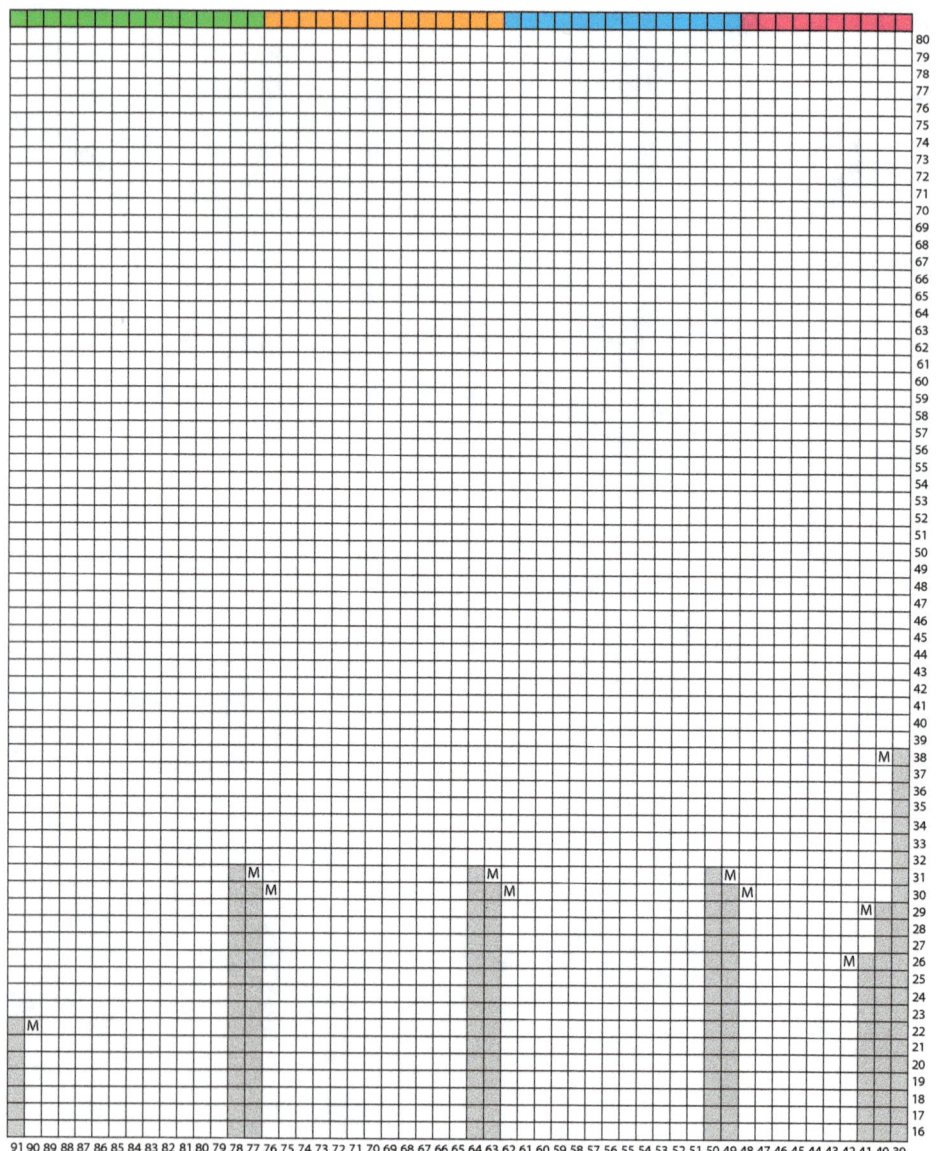

Appendix F

Blank Right Thumb Chart

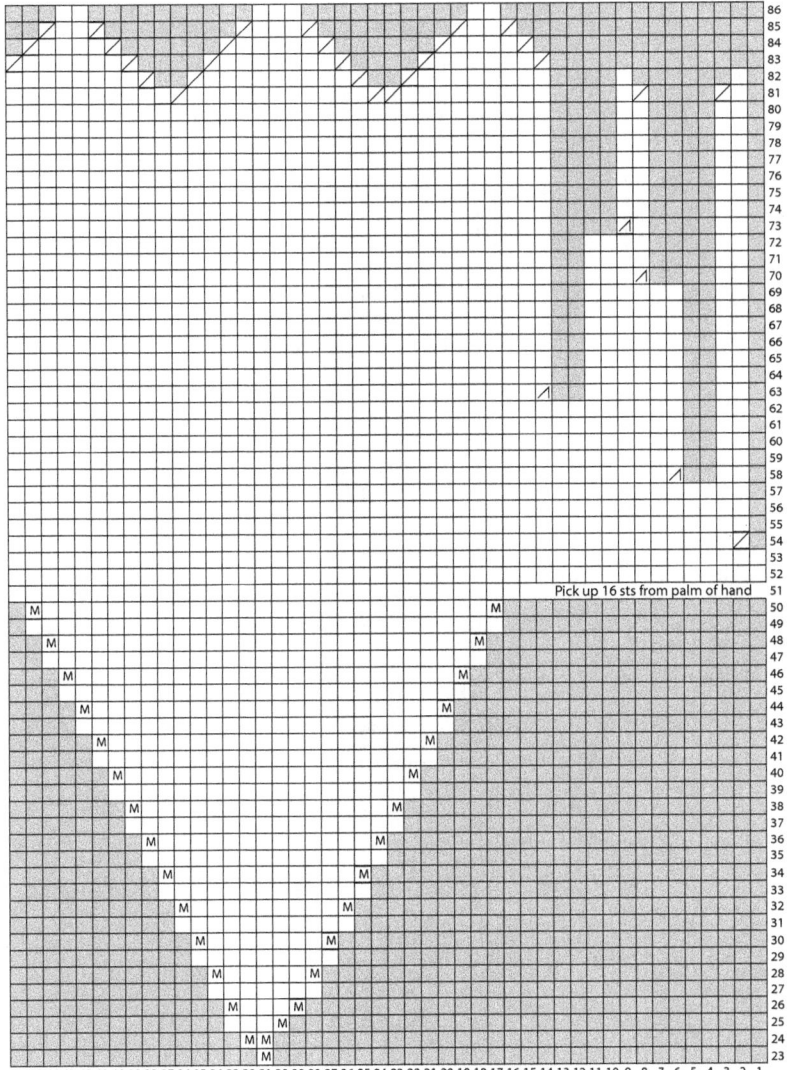

Old Hand-Knitters of the Dales

Blank Right Palm Chart

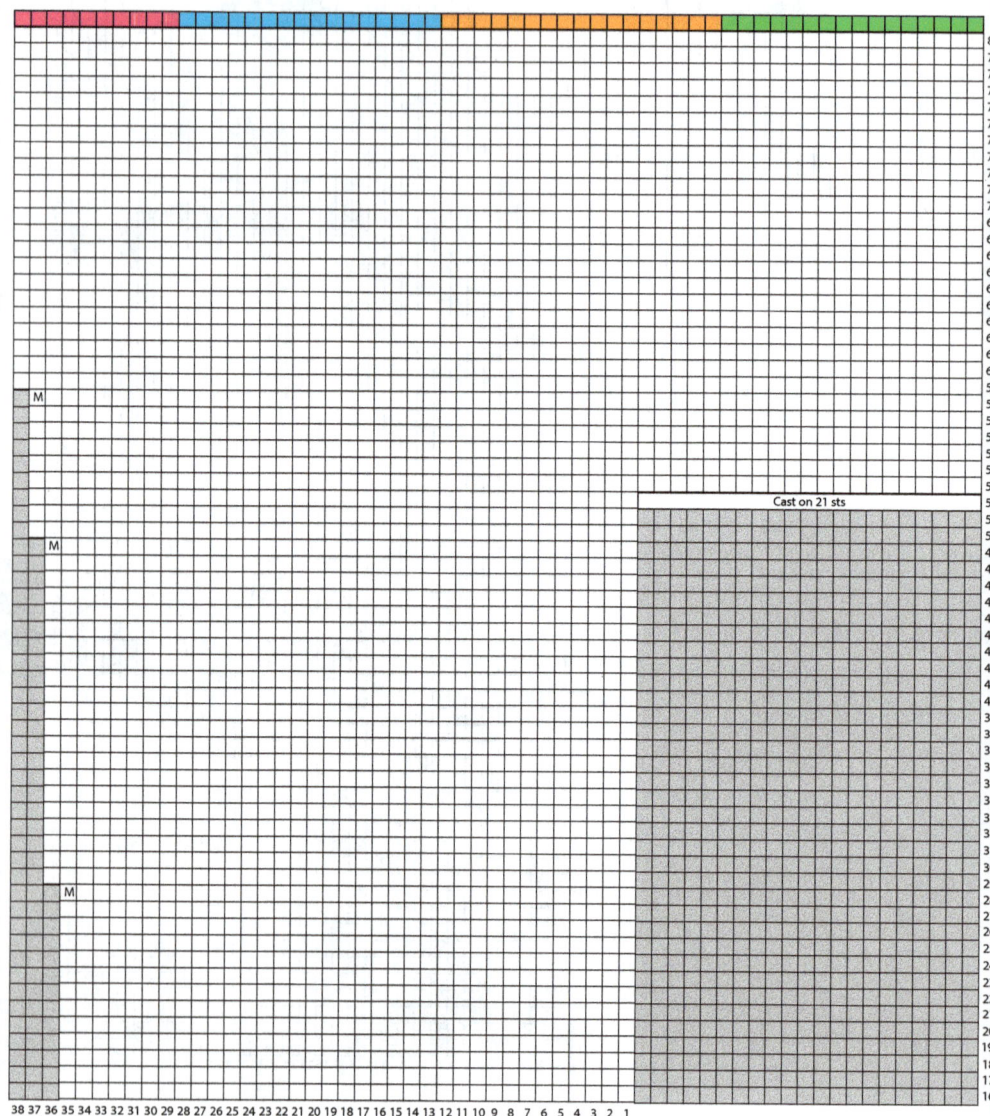

Appendix F

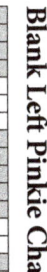
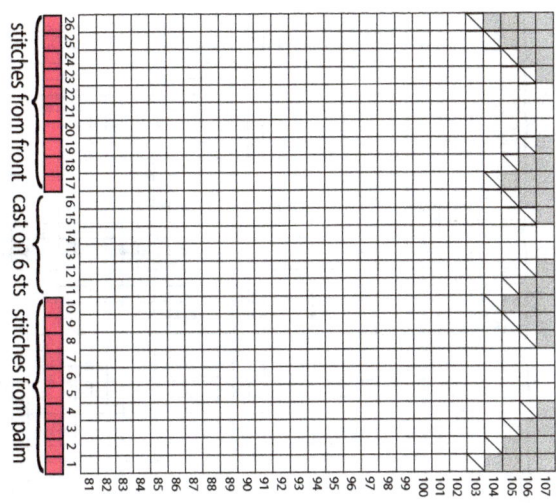

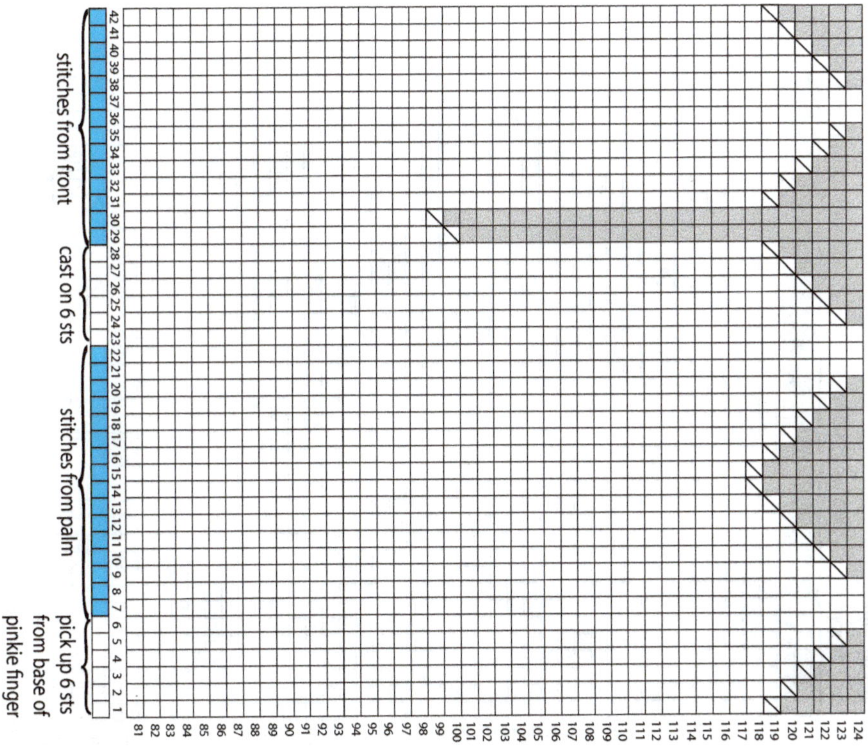

Old Hand-Knitters of the Dales

Blank Left Middle Finger Chart

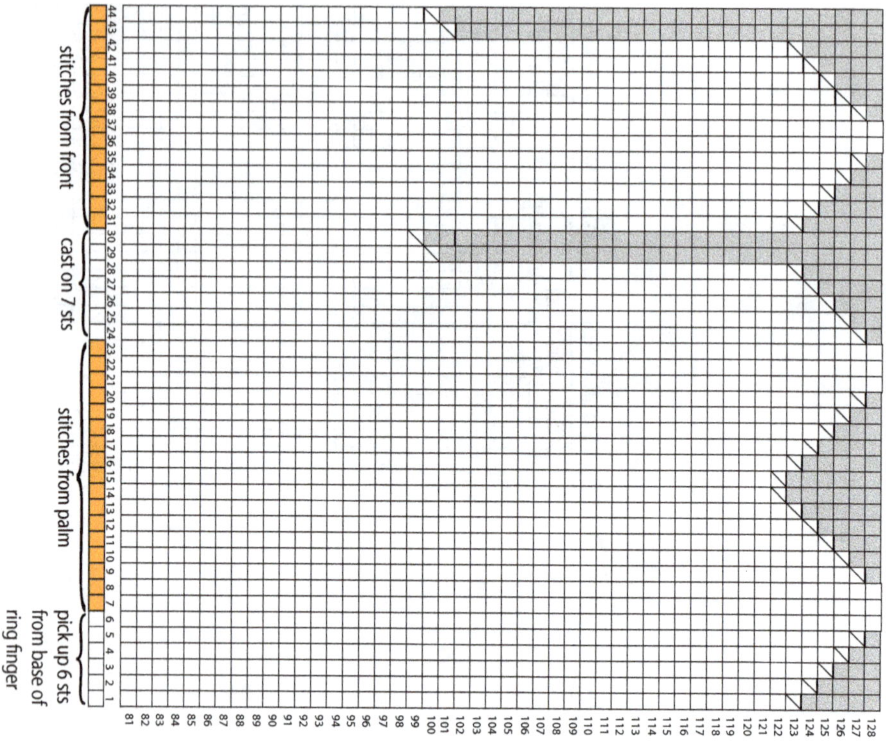

Blank Left Index Finger Chart

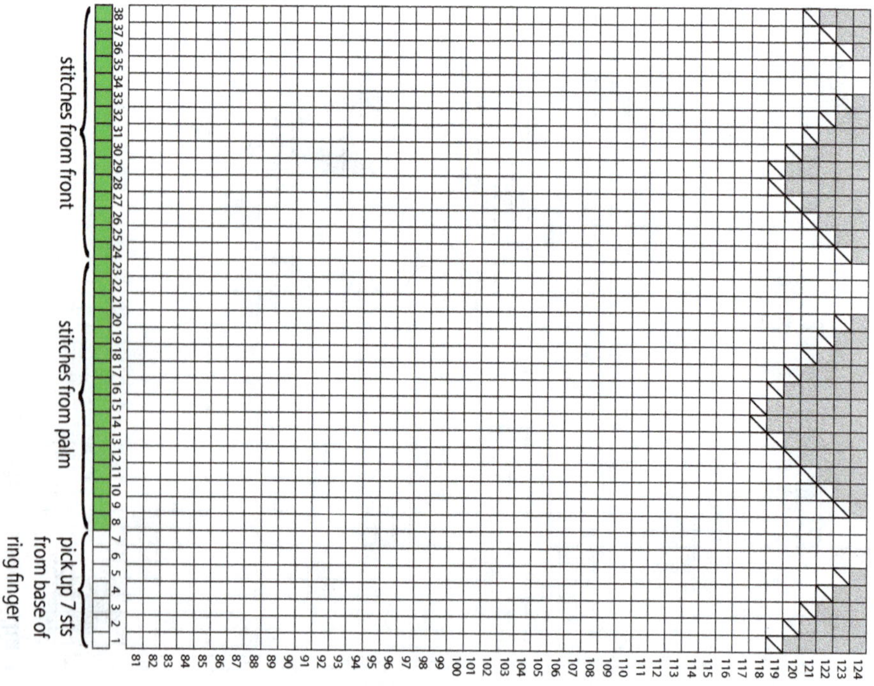

Appendix F

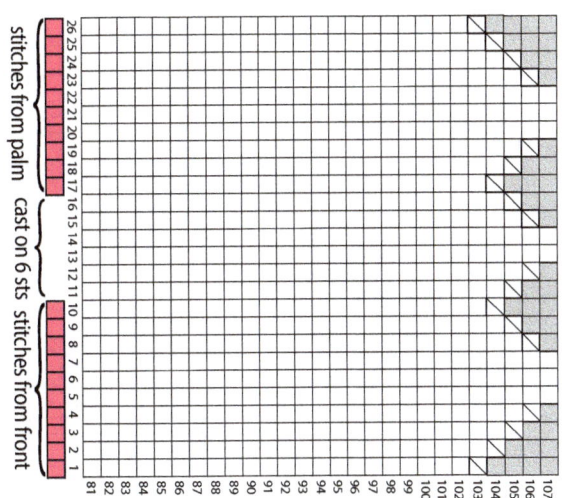

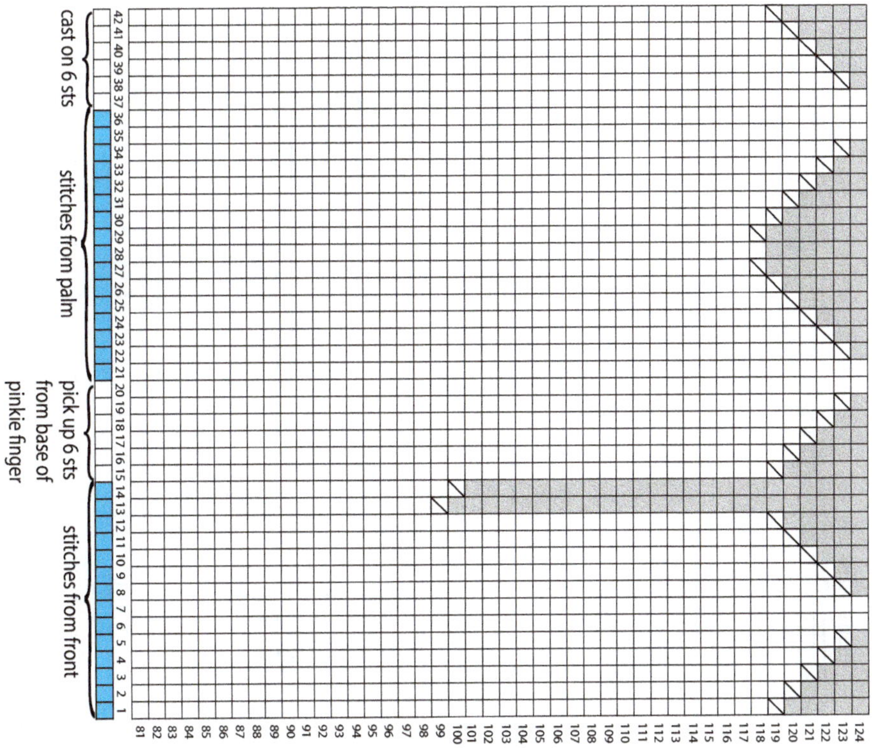

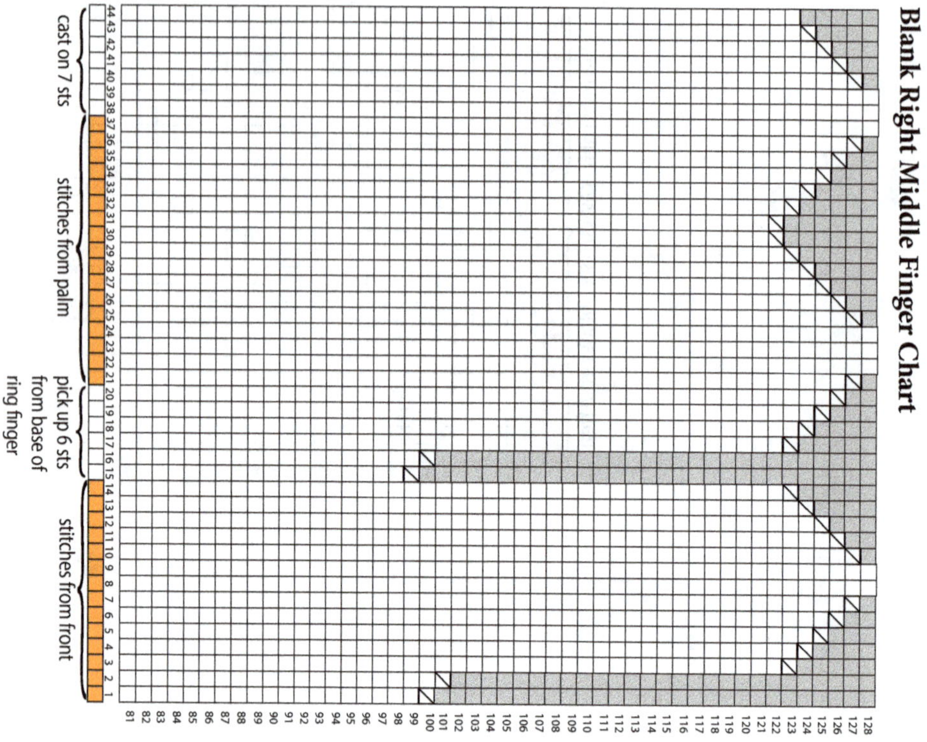

Old Hand-Knitters of the Dales

Blank Right Middle Finger Chart

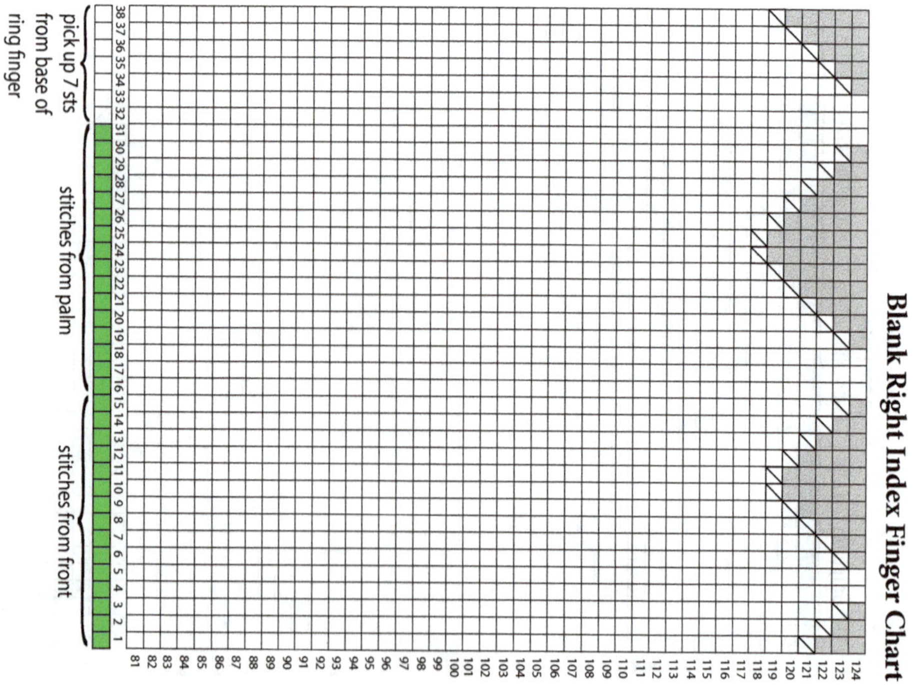

Blank Right Index Finger Chart

The hand-written tag on these beautifully preserved gloves reads: "Gloves made in Dent. Last survivor of obselete [sic] work of the 'Terrible Knitters of Dent.' Given by Mr. A. Pearson 1933." (Opposite page: palms.)

Appendix F

The tag on this equally lovely pair reads: "GLOVES. Made by Miss ALLEN of Dent given by Mrs. Inglis. 1949." (Opposite page: palms.)

Appendix F

BIBLIOGRAPHY

Knitting

Knitting Ganseys, Beth Brown-Reinsel, Interweave Press, 1993.

'Gran Taught Her To Knit at the Age of Three', Maurice Colbeck, *The Dalesman*, Vol. 57, January 1996.

The Complete Book of Traditional Guernsey and Jersey Knitting, Rae Compton, Batsford Books, 1995.

'These Daleswomen Still Use Knitting Sticks', Freda M. Douglas-Kay, *The Dalesman*, November 1956, Vol 18.

Collection of Knitting and Crochet Receipts, M. Elliot Scrivenor, 1903.

'Traditional Purls of Wisdom', Terry Fletcher, *The Dalesman*, Vol 57, June 1995, p. 58–60.

Old Hand-Knitters of the Dales, Marie Hartley and Joan Ingilby, *Dalesman*, 1951.

Quest for the Hand-Knitters, Marie Hartley and Joan Ingilby, The *Dalesman*, August 1970, p 424–6.

'Knitting in the Dales Way', Kathleen Kinder, *The Dalesman*, Vol 42, February 1981 p.908.

Knitting from the Netherlands, Henriette van der Klift-Tellegen, Dryad, 1987.

No Idle Hands: The Social History of American Knitting, Anne L. Macdonald, Ballantine Books, 1988.

Knit With Norbury, James Norbury, Odhams Press, no date, 1950s.

Traditional Knitting Patterns, James Norbury, Dover, 1962.

Traditional Knitting, Michael Pearson, Collins, 1984.

A History of Hand Knitting, Richard Rutt, Batsford, 1987.

'Love Tokens for Knitters,' Helen Simon, *Yorkshire Life*, Vol 39, No 7, Feb 1985.

Knitting from the British Islands, Alice Starmore and Anne Matheson, Bell & Hyman, 1983.

Patterns for Guernseys, Jerseys & Arans, Gladys Thompson, Dover, 1979.

Old Hand-Knitters of the Dales

'When did the Dales Knitters Begin to Knit', G. Thompson, *The Dalesman*, Vol 47, Nov 1985, p.650.

Vogue Knitting: The Ultimate Knitting Book, editors of *Vogue Knitting*, Sixth & Spring Books, 2008.

Knitting Without Tears, Elizabeth Zimmerman, Simon & Schuster, 1971.

Spinning and Textile History
The Alden Amos Big Book of Handspinning, Alden Amos, Interweave Press, 2001.

'Wonders of Yorkshire. The Life and Works of Marie Hartley and Joan Ingilby', Malcolm Barker, *The Yorkshire Journal*, Spring 1996, p. 86ff.

'The York Spinning Wheel Makers', Peter C.D. Brears, *Furniture History*, Vol XIV, 1978, 19ff.

Respect the Spindle, Abby Franquemont, Interweave Press, 2009.

High Whorling, Priscilla A. Gibson-Roberts, Nomad Press, 1998.

A Dyer's Manual, Jill Goodwin, Pelham Books, 1982.

The Yorkshire Woollen and Worsted Industries, Herbert Heaton, Oxford Clarendon Press, 1965.

The Secrets of Silk: From the Myths & Legends to the Middle Ages, Priscilla Lowry, St. John's Press, 2003.

The Secrets of Silk: From Textiles to Fashion, Priscilla Lowry, St. John's Press, 2004.

Encyclopedia of Handspinning, Mabel Ross, Batsford, 1988.

'Pioneer Memoirs from Palo Alto County', Etta May Lacey Crowder, *Iowa Journal of History and Politics* Volume 46 Issue 2, April 1948.

Maritime and Yorkshire History
Howden, an East Riding Market Town, Susan Butlers, Ken Powls, pub. Gilberdyke Local History Society.

An Account of Two Charity Schools For the Education of Girls: And of A Female Friendly Society in York. Interspersed With reflections on Charity Schools and Friendly Societies in General, Catharine Cappe, York, pub. William Blanchard, 1800.

Observations on Charity Schools, Female Friendlly Societies and Other Subjects Connected with the views of the Ladies Committee, Catharine Cappe, York, pub. Blanchard, 1805.

Bibliography

Call of the Running Tide: Girl aloft in the days of trade, Marion Carr, Maldon, 1983.

The Aire & Calder Navigation, Mike Clarke, Tempus, 1999.

Humber Shipping, Arthur G. Credland, Hull Maritime Museum, 1991.

The Yorkshire Ouse, Baron F. Duckham, David & Charles, 1967.

The Inland Waterways of East Yorkshire 1700–1900, Baron F.Duckham, East Yorkshire Local History Society, 1973.

A Life on the Humber: Keeling to Shipbuilding, Harry Fletcher, Faber & Faber, 1975.

Humber Keels, John Frank.

Yorkshire Fisherfolk, Peter Frank, Phillimore, 2002.

Superstitions and Folk Magic in Hull's Fishing Community, Alec Gill, Hutton Press, 1993.

Good Old Hessle Road, Alec Gill, Hutton Press, 1991.

The Sailing Ships and Mariners of Knottingley, Ron Gosney, Rosemary Bowyer, Ron Gosney & Sons, [no date].

Sloopmen of South Ferriby: Memoirs of Fred Harness, Cyril Harrison and T.H. Birkill, Nicholas J. Day, The Humber Keel and Sloop Preservation Society, 1996.

The Yorkshire Dales, Marie Hartley and Joan Ingilby, Aldine, 1963.

Fifty Years in the Yorkshire Dales, Marie Hartley and Joan Ingilby, Smith Settle, 1995.

Navigation on the Yorkshire Derwent, Pat Jones, The Oakwood Press, 2000.

Heritage of Patience, David Morgan Rees, Yorkshire Life, Vol. 37, February 1983.

'Marie Hartley: A Distinguished Yorkshire artist-writer in a new light', David Morgan-Rees, *The Dalesman*, Vol. 54, November 1992.

Yorkshire's River Aire, John Ogden, pub. Terence Dalton Ltd, Suffolk, 1976.

The Early History of Hull Steam Shipping, F.H.Pearson, 1896.

Humber Keels and Keelmen, Fred Schofield, Terence Dalton, Suffolk, 1988.

Prairie Smoke, Nelle Strang, unpublished MS.

Flying Sail: Humber Keels and Sloops, Michael E. Ulyatt, Mag Pye Books, 1995.

About Penelope Lister Hemingway

P ENELOPE LISTER HEMINGWAY writes for various genealogy and knitting magazines in the UK and US, and wrote *River Ganseys* for Cooperative Press (2014).

She has a degree and PGCE from The University of Birmingham, where she specialized in Old Norse and Old English, as well as eighteenth-century literature and also studied at the University of Northern Colorado. She was born in the West Riding of Yorkshire; and descends from a long line of wool weavers, and pioneers of aniline dyeing, as well as Dales knitters, farmers and inland mariners. She has five sons, and when she is not reverse engineering nineteenth-century knitting, or in an archive researching the history of knitting, can be found spinning and dyeing.

About Cooperative Press
PARTNERS IN PUBLISHING

COOPERATIVE PRESS (formerly anezka media) was founded in 2007 by Shannon Okey, a voracious reader as well as writer and editor, who had been doing freelance acquisitions work, introducing authors with projects she believed in to editors at various publishers.

Although working with traditional publishers can be very rewarding, there are some books that fly under their radar. They're too avant-garde, or the marketing department doesn't know how to sell them, or they don't think they'll sell 50,000 copies in a year.

5,000 or 50,000. Does the book matter to that 5,000? Then it should be published.

In 2009, Cooperative Press changed its named to reflect the relationships we have developed with authors working on books. We work together to put out the best quality books we can and share in the proceeds accordingly.

Thank you for supporting independent publishers and authors.

www.cooperativepress.com

www.ingramcontent.com/pod-product-compliance
Lightning Source LLC
Chambersburg PA
CBHW070547170426
43201CB00012B/1743